COMMUNICATING THE GOSPEL

Other books by William Barclay

AMBASSADOR FOR CHRIST
AND HE HAD COMPASSION
AND JESUS SAID
GOD'S YOUNG CHURCH
THE KING AND THE KINGDOM
MARCHING ORDERS
THE MEN, THE MEANING, THE MESSAGE OF THE BOOKS
THE OLD LAW AND THE NEW LAW
THE DAILY STUDY BIBLE (17 vols)

Also in this series

THE ALL-SUFFICIENT CHRIST
FLESH AND SPIRIT
TURNING TO GOD

COMMUNICATING THE GOSPEL

THE LAIRD LECTURES

WILLIAM BARCLAY

THE SAINT ANDREW PRESS
EDINBURGH

First published by The Drummond Press 1968

Republished 1978 by
THE SAINT ANDREW PRESS
121 George Street, Edinburgh

© The Trustees of the Stirling Tract Enterprise

ISBN 0 7152 0401 7

Printed and bound in Great Britain by
Bell & Bain Ltd., Glasgow

CONTENTS

PUBLISHER'S FOREWORD

The Trustees of The Stirling Tract Enterprise, having resolved to found a new series of lectures, unanimously and cordially decided to associate the new foundation with the name of Robert B. Laird, Esq., of Lynton, Kilmacolm, who has long been a most generous benefactor of the Enterprise, and keenly interested in its activities. Each course of lectures, therefore, will be known as *The Laird Lectures*.

In course of time, lecture foundations tend to exhaust every facet of relevant subject matter, and the Trustees have deliberately refrained from defining too precisely the theme, or themes, with which successive lecturers may deal. In the early years, the Trustees are interested to promote examination of the communication, exposition and defence of the Christian religion, but hold themselves free to invite consideration of other appropriate subjects.

The first series of Laird Lectures, here presented, were delivered in Stirling, in *Viewforth*, the home of Peter Drummond, the founder of The Stirling Tract Enterprise, and now the offices of the County Council of Stirling. The Trustees greatly appreciate the very great kindness of the County officials in granting the necessary permission, in the most generous arrangements they made, and in their warm personal interest in the occasion.

While these first lectures were delivered in Stirling,

where the Enterprise was founded, the Trustees will readily consider the suitability of other places.

The Trustees deem themselves fortunate indeed that Professor William Barclay was able to accept their invitation to give the first series of lectures, and on a subject in which he has for so long shown himself pre-eminent. They warmly thank him for so successfully inaugurating the new foundation.

PREFACE

I should be sadly lacking in courtesy if I did not express my deep appreciation of the honour given to me in entrusting me with the task of delivering the first series of Laird Lectures; and I should like to thank the people at Stirling for their welcome and for their kindness to me when the lectures were being delivered. It was a special joy to me that Mr. Laird himself was able to be at the first of them. I owe a special debt to the Revd. Andrew McCosh of The Stirling Tract Enterprise for making such magnificent arrangements, for all his graciousness and efficiency combined, and for his patience with me while this manuscript was being prepared.

The first three chapters contain the Laird Lectures, the fourth chapter consists of a lecture given to a joint audience of Protestants and Roman Catholics in a series of lectures arranged by the Extra-Mural Department of the University.

I send out this book with the hope and the prayer that it may do something to help the communication of the Gospel in the 20th century.

WILLIAM BARCLAY.

University of Glasgow.

CHAPTER I

COMMUNICATING THE GOSPEL IN THE PROPHETS

IT IS CERTAINLY true to say that no body of men ever left their mark on the spiritual history of mankind as did the Hebrew prophets of the 8th and the 7th centuries before Christ. It may be recklessly to attempt the impossible to try to set out the characteristics of their communication in one single lecture; but any such attempt will have one virtue. It will save us from getting lost in detail, and will enable us to take a panoramic view of their teaching, and it will compel us to concentrate on the essentials of their message.

They were men of curiously mixed background. Amos came from Tekoa, on the very edge of the Judaean desert. He was a herdsman and a dresser of sycamore trees (*Amos 7. 14*). The sycamore tree bore a coarse fig; it had to be nipped, or bruised, to hasten its ripening, and this was what Amos did. He was a man with no theological background, a man who had met God, not in the schools or the cities, but in the wide open spaces. Isaiah was a city-dweller who lived and worked and preached in the city of Jerusalem. Jeremiah was from a priestly family from the village of Anathoth, which was two and a half miles north-east of Jerusalem. He was trained in the traditions of his fathers and came from the religious aristocracy of his nation. The man from the wide-open spaces, the man from the city streets, the man from the family of priests— each had his message and each had his part to play. There

1

is no one mould into which the man of God must be cast.

It may well be that the first thing that strikes a modern reader about the prophets is that they lived in a different kind of world from the world of twentieth century man, for they lived in a world which was the arena of the action of God.

To the prophets, nature was the instrument of the action of God. Disobedience to God brought the blight and the mildew and the locust to ruin their crops, the pestilence and the disaster (*Amos 4. 10-12*). The Deuteronomist is very definite. If men will not obey God, ' The Lord will smite you with consumption and with fever, inflammation and fiery heat, and with drought and with blasting, and with mildew. They shall pursue you till you perish. And the heavens over your head shall be brass, and the earth under you shall be iron. The Lord will make the rain of your land powder and dust; from heaven it shall come down upon you until you are destroyed ' (*Deuteronomy 28. 22-24*). Nature to the prophets was the instrument of God's judgment.

Equally, to the prophets history was the arena of the action of God. The nations, whether they knew it or not, were his agents. When victory came to Israel, the victor was God; and when defeat came to Israel, it was the punishment of God in operation.

One principle operates here, and it is a principle which must be understood before the world in which the prophets lived can be understood. It is very significant that in the Jewish division of the Canon of Scripture what we call the historical books are called by the Jews the former prophets. In other words, history was to them the word of God proclaimed in events. But the principle which is all-important is this — *to the Jewish mind there was no such thing as secondary causes.* Everything was traceable to the direct action of God. If there is a storm or a drought, we explain it in terms of certain causes, atmospheric conditions which we can identify and describe. If there is a famine or pestilence, we explain it as being due to certain quite identifiable causes and physical and scientific laws. But the Jew said quite simply, God sent the rain; God thundered; God blasted the earth and its crops; God sent the pestilence. The secondary cause is eliminated and God becomes the moving cause.

There is one vivid example of this in the second Book of Kings. In the nineteenth chapter we have an incident of which, very unusually, we have parallel accounts in secular historians. The incident comes from the siege of Jerusalem by Sennacherib. It seemed that the fate of Jerusalem was sealed and settled and that there was nothing to do but to await the inevitable end; and then against all expectation Sennacherib, when he seemed to have the city in his hands, suddenly left and returned to Assyria. The Hebrew historian tells the story as follows:

'And that night the angel of the Lord went forth, and slew a hundred and eighty-five thousand in the camp of the Assyrians; and when men arose early in the morning, behold these were all dead bodies. Then Sennacherib king of Assyria departed, and went home and dwelt at Nineveh' (*2 Kings 19, 35, 36*).

There the action is ascribed to the angel of the Lord, for God had said:

' I will defend this city to save it, for my own sake and for the sake of my servant David ' (2 *Kings* 19. 34).

Now it so happens that this story is told by Herodotus, the Greek historian, from the Egyptian point of view, and in that version the panic-stricken flight of the Assyrians is attributed to the fact that mice gnawed the strings of their bows and the thongs of their shields. So then in the Egyptian version of the story the defeat of the Assyrians was due to the action of mice. But there is a third version of this story in the works of Berosus, a Chaldaean historian, and he quite simply says that Sennacherib had to withdraw because his army was decimated by plague. Which story is right? Surely the answer is that all three are right. The modern version would be that Sennacherib's army was destroyed by an outbreak of bubonic plague, which is carried by mice and rats. The Chaldaean historian says: Plague did it. The Egyptian story says: Mice did it. The Hebrew story says: God did it.

To understand the prophets at all we must clearly remember that for them nature is the instrument of God and history is the arena of the action of God.

There is a sense in which we can no longer look at things with this kind of world view; but there is also a sense in which we would do well to return to this world view, for we are in a position today when our relation to nature is that nature may well turn and rend us, and we are in a position when the events of history may well be man's ruin—unless man to his knowledge adds reverence, and unless man's control of power is matched by his fitness to control it. This much is true that the safe use of power depends on obedience to the laws of God, for ultimately this is a moral universe—and that is precisely the prophetic point of view.

We may next look at the things against which the prophets mainly did battle.

The first battle was against *idolatry*. It may be that we in the twentieth century find idolatry very difficult to understand; we may find it difficult to understand how even a primitive man could worship a piece of stone or wood or metal, however beautifully worked or carved. But the beginning of idolatry was very simple and natural and very understandable. It was hard, as it were, to worship nothingness, and the idol was simply an attempt to make the god visible, or to provide the god with a place wherein to dwell. Just as a person might find it easier to write a letter to an absent friend with a photograph of the absent one in front of him, so men felt that it was easier to worship the unseen god with a kind of pictorial representation of him there in front of them. But inevitably that which began by being an aid to worship came itself to be worshipped, and that which was no more than a kind of reminder of the god became itself divine.

The main weapon which the prophets used against idolatry was scorn. They drew, always with vividness, and sometimes with Homeric laughter, the contrast between the dead idol and the living God. Isaiah draws the picture of the man choosing his tree, cutting it down, working at it with line and hammer and saw and chisel. He sees him

5

using some of the wood to light a fire to warm his house and cook his dinner, and some of the wood to make his god.

> 'Half of it he burns in the fire; over the half he eats flesh, he roasts meat and is satisfied; also he warms himself and says, Aha, I am warm, I have seen the fire! And the rest he makes into a god his idol; and falls down to it and worships it; he prays to it and says, Deliver me, for thou art my god!' (*Isaiah 44. 9-17*).

He draws the picture of the helpless god, fixed in the one place, carried laboriously about on men's shoulders, if it has to be moved (*Isaiah 46. 5-7*). Jeremiah talks of the gods that are nailed together with hammers (*Jeremiah 10. 3-5*). Again and again the prophets speak of the gods which have mouths and cannot speak, and eyes and cannot see, and ears and cannot hear (*Deuteronomy 4. 28; Psalm 135. 15-17; Isaiah 40. 18-20; 37. 18, 19*).

To this day there is a spiritual idolatry possible. There is the case of the congregation which so worships its own stone and lime that it will not contemplate union with another congregation, even when that union is clearly for the good of the Church. Basically, idolatry is the worship of things; it is the worship of that which man has created rather than of him who has created man. It may well be true that no age in history has worshipped things to the extent that this present age does. The measure of success, the height of a man's prestige, is measured by the number of things that he has succeeded in acquiring. If idolatry be essentially the worship of things, then idolatry is as prevalent today as ever it was.

The second battle that the prophets consistently fought was the battle against *syncretism*.

Religion passed through three stages. The first stage was *polytheism*; at this stage there were believed to be many gods. The sun and the moon and the fire and the sea and all kinds of things and powers were personified into gods. The second stage was *henotheism*; at this stage men still believed that there were many gods, but they also believed that for them there was only one god. At this stage each nation had its god; within the territory of the nation the god was supreme, but his power did not go beyond the national territory. So we find Jephthah saying to the Ammonites: 'Will you not possess what Chemosh your god gives you to possess? And all that Jahweh our God has dispossessed before us we will possess' (*Judges 11. 24*). For the Ammonites Chemosh was God, for the Israelites Jahweh was God, each supreme in his own territory. The third stage is *monotheism*; at this stage there comes the belief that there is only one God who is the God of all the earth.

Now the trouble in prophetic times was that henotheism was far from being dead; there was still the feeling that each land had its own god, and that within the confines of that land that god must be respected. When Israel came into Palestine, the land already had its gods for it already had its inhabitants. These gods were the Baals. Now the characteristic of these Canaanite gods was that they were fertility gods and goddesses. They stood for the power of life and of growth. They stood for the power which made the corn and the grape and the olive

7

swell and ripen. Now the supreme fertility power is the power of sex, and so these gods stand for sexual fertility.

Their worship very naturally involved the glorification of their gifts; it therefore led to feasting and to drunkenness. Above all, it led to the view of the sexual act as an act of worship; and so their temples and their shrines were all equipped with staffs of sacred priestesses who were really sacred prostitutes, and worship was a kind of ceremonial and ritual intercourse with them.

It was because of all this that the prophets had that horror of Baal worship which runs all through their works. A people naturally superstitious still had the haunting feeling that they might be better to make their peace with the gods of the land. Any people naturally passionate would find in this fertility worship something which had a burning attraction. Hosea hears God say:

'And she (Israel) did not know
that it was I who gave her
the grain, the wine and the oil,
and who lavished upon her silver
and gold which they used for Baal' (*Hosea 2. 8*).

The people wanted a religious syncretism in which they could worship Jahweh and at the same time maintain their contact with the fertility gods and goddesses and their worship.

Once again, the situation is not entirely remote, for it simply and basically means that the religion which is to survive is the religion which refuses to compromise with its environment and which worships God and God alone.

It is time now to come to the main emphasis of the

prophetic message. The consistent and passionate message of the prophets is that no amount of ritual and no amount of ceremony can replace ethical conduct. Liturgy can be magnificent; sacrifice can be munificent; it is useless and worthless and unavailing, if it is regarded as a substitute for life and living. Cultic magnificence without ethical living is a vast irrelevance. It is useless to think that a man or a nation can discharge its or his duties to God through the splendour of a temple with its sacrifices and its ritual and its liturgy; that duty can only be expressed in terms of love of God and love of man; and the essence of the whole matter is that no one can ever prove that he loves God except by loving men.

It is in this emphasis that we find so many of the greatest passages of the prophets.

'When you appear before me,
     who requires of you this trampling of my courts?
Bring no more vain offerings;
     incense is an abomination to me.
New moon and sabbath and the calling of assemblies—
     I cannot endure iniquity and solemn assembly.
Your new moons and your appointed feasts
     my soul hates;
they have become a burden to me,
     I am weary of bearing them.
When you spread forth your hands,
     I will hide my eyes from you;
even though you make many prayers,
     I will not listen;
     your hands are full of blood.

Wash yourselves; make yourselves clean;
>   remove the evil of your doings
>   from before my eyes;
cease to do evil;
>   learn to do good;
seek justice;
>   correct oppression;
defend the fatherless,
>   plead for the widow' (*Isaiah 1. 12-17*).

Jeremiah pours his scorn on those who think that they are safe because they possess the temple of the Lord.

'Will you steal, murder, commit adultery, swear falsely, burn incense to Baal, and go after other gods that you have not known, and then come and stand before me in this house, which is called after my name, and say: We are delivered!' (*Jeremiah 7. 8-10*).

We have the same grim emphasis in Amos:

'I hate, I despise your feasts,
>   and I take no delight in your solemn assemblies.
Even though you offer me burnt-offerings and cereal
>   offerings,
>   I will not accept them,
and the peace offerings of your fatted beasts
>   I will not look upon.
Take away from me the noise of your songs;
>   to the melody of your harps I will not listen.
But let justice roll down like waters,
>   and righteousness like an ever-flowing stream'
>   (*Amos 5. 21-24*).

Perhaps most famous of all is the passage of Micah:

'With what shall I come before the Lord,
   and bow myself before God on high?
Shall I come before him with burnt offerings,
   with calves a year old?
Will the Lord be pleased with thousands of rams,
   and with ten thousands of rivers of oil?
Shall I give my firstborn for my transgression,
   the fruit of the body for the sin of my soul?
He has showed you, O man, what is good;
   and what does the Lord require of you
But to do justice and to love kindness,
   and to walk humbly with your God?'(*Micah 6. 6-8*).

The most elaborate and costly worship in the world cannot take the place of the life of obedience to God. Hosea summed it up:

'For I desire steadfast love and not sacrifice;
   the knowledge of God rather than burnt offerings
      (*Hosea 6. 6*).

There is in the prophets this terrific moral earnestness, this insistence that nothing can take the place of life.

There is more here, much more, than meets the eye. The Greek word for pure is *katharos*. In Leviticus, for instance, in the Septuagint, *katharos* occurs more than thirty times, and never once in the sense of moral purity; it is always used in the sense of ritual purity, of cleanness in the ritual and the ceremonial sense of the term, the purity which comes from the performance of the right washings and the observance of the correct tabus. It was this which aroused the holy fury of the prophets.

It may be thought that this is something which we

have overpassed, and that this is an error into which we are not likely to fall. But the Church is not free of this yet. It is possible still to love systems even more than we love God, and so to exalt an ecclesiastical system that the wider aims of unity are forgotten. It is possible to be so in love with ritual perfection and liturgical correctness that these things become identified with worship and even with religion. Bentley the great classical scholar used to insist that we must never get so immersed in the minutiae of grammar and the like that we lose sight of the *res ipsa*, the thing itself. And the Church has never escaped the danger of worshipping systems even more than it worshipped God.

This insistence on the ethical nature of religion turned the prophets towards two things. First, it meant that they were intensely interested in politics. The prophets certainly did not believe that the man of God is not interested in politics; on the contrary, they believed that the man of God must be interested and involved in the political situation. If history is the arena in which the will of God is being worked out, then clearly the man of God must be involved in its events.

The time of the prophets was a time when the Middle East was in a seething ferment. There was the contest between Assyria and Babylon; and there was always the contest between whoever held power in the north and Egypt in the south. Palestine was always caught between the world Empires.

Péguy, the French philosopher, said that everything worthwhile begins in mysticism and ends in politics, and the prophets were sure that the vision of God had to be worked out in events. They therefore took it upon themselves to rebuke kings and rulers and to insist that the nation must depend not on foreign alliances but on fidelity to God. When Niemoller spoke to Hitler about the anxiety that he and the Church felt about the situation in Germany, Hitler's answer was, 'You look after the Church and leave such things to me.' And the consequences were disastrous.

But this insistence on the ethical quality of real religion was not confined to the wider world of politics. It dominated the whole life of Israel as the prophets saw it, down to the smallest detail. To the prophets social justice was something which was part and parcel of everyday life. It was something by which the rights of the ordinary man were protected, and the arrogance of the rich condemned.

There are two things which specially show how all pervasive this social justice was in the mind of the prophets. One of the extraordinary things about the Bible is the number of times it insists on honest weights and measures. ' You shall have just balances, just weights,' says the law (*Leviticus 19. 36*). ' You shall not have in your bag two kinds of weights, a large and a small. You shall not have in your house two kinds of measures, a large and a small. A full and just weight you shall have, a full and just measure you shall have, that your days may be prolonged in the land which the Lord your God gives you ' (*Deuteronomy 24. 13-15*). ' A false balance is an abomination to the Lord,' says the Sage, ' but a just weight is his delight ' (*Proverbs 11. 1*). ' A just balance and scales are the Lord's;

all the weights in the bag are his work ' (*Proverbs* 16. 11; 20. 10, 23).

So integrated into life is this social justice that even the weights and measures of everyday are the concern of God.

Zechariah has a wonderful picture (*Zechariah* 14. 20, 21). One of the great possessions of Israel was the golden vessels, nearly a hundred of them, which were used in the Temple every day in the daily sacrifice; they were holy to the Lord. One of the most splendid things in the Temple worship was the robe of the High Priest; it was bordered round the foot with seventy little golden bells, and they, too, were holy to the Lord. On his forehead the High Priest wore the gold plate with the words ' Holy to the Lord ' on it. But Zechariah says that when the day comes when God really rules among men, even the common bells on the horses' harness, and even the pots and the pans in every kitchen in the land will be holy to the Lord. The prophets insisted on the sanctification of common life.

There are certain other aspects of the prophetic thought at which we must look. To anyone reading the prophetic message one fact stands out. The prophetic message is to the nation. It is the nation which will be rewarded for fidelity and it is the nation which will meet disaster for disobedience. It is not until Ezekiel that the individual emerges: ' The soul that sins shall die ' (*Ezekiel* 18. 4).

The prophetic idea of the nation as the unit has often been made a ground of criticism; but it is strange to see how right the prophets were. It is in fact one of the tragedies of the present situation that so often people do not think in terms of the community and of the nation. They think in terms of a sectional interest and even of an individual interest. The phrase, 'I'm all right, Jack,' has become a kind of summary of the attitude of people to life in general. It took a long time to discover the individual, but it may well be said what that is needed today is a rediscovery of the nation and of the community, and a realisation that a man cannot live to himself or die to himself. It has to be rediscovered that the individual is part of the nation, and that unless he realises that there is an interest beyond his own interest and the interest of his own trade or class, the consequences can and must be disastrous. Men no longer need to be taught to think individually; they need to be taught to think nationally. The prophetic conviction that the nation flourishes or perishes as a unit is something which this age needs to relearn.

But the vision of the prophets went far beyond the nation. The vision of the prophets was a vision of the world. The Jews always thought of themselves as the chosen nation and always believed that they had a special and peculiar place among the nations of the world. But all through their history they interpreted this in two different ways. Often, perhaps most often, they interpreted this in terms of privilege, and they saw themselves as the masters and the conquerors of the world. And even in the prophets this line of thought comes out. 'Those who strive against you shall be as nothing and shall perish' (Isaiah 41. 11).

'For the nation and kingdom
  that will not serve you shall perish;
  those nations shall be utterly laid waste'
                              (*Isaiah* 60. 12).

'Thus says the Lord,
  The wealth of Egypt and the merchandise of Ethiopia,
    and Sabeans men of stature,
  shall come over to you and be yours,
    they shall follow you;
      they shall come over in chains and bow down to
        you'   (*Isaiah* 45. 14).

The dream of world mastery was a dream that did not die. But there was a far nobler dream than that, and in the prophets that dream appears. It was the vision that Israel was chosen, not for privilege, but for responsibility, and that she had a duty to discharge to the whole world, and that duty was to lead men to God and to the truth.

'I am the Lord, and I have called you in righteousness,
    I have taken you by the hand and kept you;
  I have given you as a covenant to the people,
    a light to the nations' (*Isaiah* 42. 6).

'I will give you as a light to the nations,
    that my salvation may reach to the end of the
      earth' (*Isaiah* 49. 6).

'They shall declare my glory among the nations'
                              (*Isaiah* 66. 19).

The life of Israel was to be such that it would be impossible not to see that she possessed a secret which others did not possess, but which they could not but covet. So Zechariah (8. 20-23) paints the picture:

'Thus says the Lord of hosts: People shall yet come, even the inhabitants of many cities; the inhabitants of one city shall go to another saying: Let us go at once to entreat the favour of the Lord, and to seek the Lord of hosts; I am going. Many peoples and strong nations shall come to seek the Lord of hosts in Jerusalem, and to entreat the favour of the Lord. Thus says the Lord of hosts: In those days ten men from the nations of every tongue shall take hold of the robe of a Jew saying: Let us go with you, for we have heard that God is with you.'

There would be that in the life of a Jew which by the very sight of it would invite men to God.

Here is a great and an enduring thought. The greatness of a nation lies not in privilege and in power, but in the acceptance of responsibility to the world. The function of a great nation is not to hoard privileges but to share them, not to keep other nations down but to lift them up, not to make them subjects but to make them partners in the life of the world.

But the vision of the prophets went beyond this earth altogether. A basic part of the belief of the prophets was the belief in the Two Ages. There was this present age which is an evil age. There was the age to come which is the golden age of the Kingdom of God. But the question was, How was the one to turn into the other? How was the age of evil to become the age of good? Of one thing the prophets were certain—human resources are inadequate

to effect this change. So they looked for the direct intervention of God, the time when God would break into
history and would by his own divine action make his
kingdom come. And they called the time of that intervention the Day of the Lord. The prophets are full of the
idea of the Day of the Lord, and always there is in it power
and terror.

'Behold, the day of the Lord comes,
    cruel, with wrath and fierce anger,
To make the earth a desolation
    and to destroy the sinners from it.' (*Isaiah 13. 9*).

'The day of the Lord is great and very terrible;
    who can endure it?' (*Joel 2. 11*).

It is the great and terrible day of the Lord (*Joel 2, 30*).

'Woe to you who desire the day of the Lord!
    Why would you have the day of the Lord?
It is darkness and not light' (*Amos 5. 18*).

'The great day of the Lord is near and hastening fast;
The sound of the day of the Lord is bitter,
    the mighty man cries aloud there.
A day of wrath is that day,
    a day of distress and anguish,
A day of ruin and devastation,
    a day of darkness and gloom,
    a day of clouds and thick darkness'
                                (*Zephaniah 1. 14, 15*).

In Malachi also it is the great and terrible day of the Lord
(*Malachi 4. 5*).

18

The day of the Lord had three great characteristics. It was to come suddenly and without warning; it was to involve the disintegration of the very fabric of the world as it now is; it was to be a day of God's final judgment; and it was to result in a new and lovely world, the world of God.

This is not science and literalism; this is vision and poetry; but in it there are three abiding truths.

First, it teaches that God has not left the world to itself; the directing hand is ultimately still his.

Second, history is not a road that is leading nowhere; history is leading to a goal and a climax and a dénouement.

Third, this world is not destined for destruction and annihilation but for recreation.

The belief in the Day of the Lord is not the result of pessimism, based on the belief in a godless world; it is the result of that optimism which believes in the ultimate victory of God.

There is one other prophetic picture at which we must look, for it is a picture which has the very heart of Jewish religion in it, and yet it has produced ways of speaking which sound strange to modern ears. The prophets look upon the relationship between God and his people as a marriage relationship. Israel is the bride of God and God is the husband of Israel. Isaiah writes (62. 5):

'As the bridegroom rejoices over the bride,
      so shall your God rejoice over you.'

'Your Maker is your husband,
      the Lord of hosts is his name' (*Isaiah* 54. 5).

So Jeremiah can look on the period when God led Israel

through the wilderness as the honeymoon period in the relationship between God and Israel.

'I remember the devotion of your youth,
  your love as a bride,
how you followed me in the wilderness,
  in a land not sown' (*Jeremiah* 2. 2).

The importance of this is that it lifts the relationship of God and Israel clean out of the realm of law; it removes it from the sphere of master and servant, or even of king and subject; it makes it the relationship of lover and loved one.

It is this picture which has brought into biblical language two pictures which, as we have said, are strange to modern ears. This is why, when Israel turned away from God, the people are said to go a-whoring after strange gods, or, as the RSV translates it, the people are said to play the harlot after strange gods. ' Then his people will rise and play the harlot after the strange gods of the land, where they go to be among them, and they will forsake me and break my covenant which I have made with them,' says God to Moses before Moses' death (*Deuteronomy* 31. 16: cp. *Judges* 2. 17; 8. 27, 33; *Hosea* 9. 1).

When the people are unfaithful to God, it is not only the breach of a contract, or a bargain, or an agreement; it is a sin against love. It is infidelity; it is unfaithfulness of the loved one to the lover. In other words, when men abandon God and take their own way, they do not so much break God's law as they break God's heart.

It is from this, too, that we get the idea of God being a jealous God, an idea which once again sounds strange to

modern ears. ' I, the Lord your God, am a jealous God '
(*Exodus* 20. 5; 34. 14; *Deuteronomy* 5. 9; 6. 15). ' The Lord
is a jealous God and avenging ' (*Nahum* 1. 2). The idea is
simply that a lover can share his loved one with no one;
love means exclusively to possess and exclusively to be
possessed. The jealousy of God of which the Old Testament
speaks is the passionate love of the lover, who has given
his all, and who therefore demands the loved one's all.
The divine human relationship moves not in the realm of
law, but in the realm of love.

It remains to look at one last side of the prophetic
message. We have looked at the substance of the message;
we must end by looking at the method of the message.
About this there are two things to be said.

First, quite simply, the prophets were masters of
words. Whatever their message may be, they have their
place for ever among the world's great masters of literature
and of the word. J. Muilenburg says in his article on *Isaiah*
in the revised one-volume Hastings' *Dictionary of the
Bible*:

> ' We think of Isaiah as one of the great prophets of
> Israel, but he was also a poet of stature . . . Despite
> the vigour and passion of his speech, he maintains an
> elevation, indeed a grandeur and a prophetic
> eloquence, a restraint and rhythmic control, a kind
> of loftiness and elegance of speech, seldom if ever
> surpassed . . . His literary forms and types are almost
> as varied as his images; invectives and threats are most
> common, but songs, dirges, laments, mocking songs
> and hymns are also present. Like the prophets before

21

and after him, Isaiah places all this extraordinary
wealth of literary composition at the service of
prophecy.'

Apart altogether from his message, Isaiah was one of the
great literary craftsmen of the world.

The same writer, writing in the same work, says of
Jeremiah:

'It is clear that in Jeremiah we are looking into the
face of a poet of extraordinary sensitivity, a man with
a seeing eye and a hearing ear, quickly responsive to
all that went on about him, with a rare ability to
express in moving language all that he had observed
and felt and suffered, all that he had heard from
Jahweh. His poetry . . . is unrivalled in the records of
Semitic antiquity in the intensity of its lyricism, its
dramatic power, its abundance of memorable images,
its sensuousness and passionateness, its immediacy of
response to every mood of nature, and every nuance
of the soul of man.'

James Paterson reminds us how it was said of a man who
had the magic of words that his words ' became alive and
walked up and down in the hearts of his hearers.' To the
Hebrew, a word was 'fearfully alive.' It was not simply
a sound; it was 'a unit of energy charged with power.'
The blessing given by Isaac to Jacob (*Genesis 27*), even if
obtained by a trick, can never be recalled. The word of
God has such power that it is like a hammer that breaks
the rock in pieces. (*Jeremiah 23. 29*). The Hebrew was
careful with words. He had to be for Hebrew has fewer
than 10,000 words while Greek has more than 200,000.

There is something which is not insignificant here. To the great prophets only the finest language was sufficient for the finest thought. They loved words and used them lovingly like artists. It may be, it may well be, that at least some of the impact of the Christian message today is lost because of the careless and slovenly way in which it is presented. It is frequently said now that the day of the orator in the pulpit is over, and that nowadays the style of preaching must be colloquial and conversational. It is now almost the exception for a preacher to write his sermons. It is well to remember that the greatest preachers the ancient world ever knew were men who worked as hard on their words as they did on their message.

But second, the prophets had a method of delivering their message which was deliberately designed to startle their hearers. Sometimes the prophets came to feel that words were useless, that they simply did not penetrate, that the hearts of the people were so fat, their ears so heavy, their eyes so shut (*Isaiah 6. 10*) that the word could achieve nothing. To meet this situation they worked out a system of what is known as *dramatic prophetic action*. Instead of *saying* something, they *did* something, as if to say, If you will not listen, you will look. When ear-gate was closed, they made their assault by way of eye-gate.

Ahijah (*I Kings 11. 26-37*) wished to make the political situation clear to the people. He wished to tell them that Rehoboam's reckless conduct was going to split the nation and that ten of the tribes were going to revolt to Jeroboam and only two remain faithful to Rehoboam. So Ahijah put on a new robe. He went out and he met Jeroboam.

He snatched off the robe; tore it into twelve pieces; handed ten to Jeroboam and kept two for himself. ' That,' he said, ' is what is going to happen to this people.' People may not listen to a man's words, but when he starts to strip in the middle of the main street they will certainly stop to see what is going on.

Isaiah wished to tell the people that they would be conquered by Babylon and by Nebuchadnezzar. It was a message to which they simply refused to listen; they were too busy engineering the political alliances which were to save them. So Isaiah made himself yokes and thongs and went about the streets wearing them. Naturally people asked him what he was doing. ' This,' he said, ' is what is going to happen to the nation and to you ' (*Isaiah 27. 1-7*).

Jeremiah wished to show the people where their infidelity was leading, and they would not listen. He got a waistcloth; he wore it; after a time he took and buried it in the mud of the banks of the Euphrates; he left it there for days; then he went and dug it up again all soiled and spoiled. ' This,' he said as a message from God, ' is what is going to happen to this people. As a waistcloth clings to the waist of a man, this people were meant to cling to me. But they have left me, and, as this waistcloth is ruined, so will they be ' (*Jeremiah 13. 1-11*).

The greatest master of all of the dramatic prophetic action was Ezekiel. On a brick he made a model of the fall and the siege of a city. ' This,' he said, ' is what will happen to Jerusalem ' (*Ezekiel 4. 1-3*). His book is littered with such actions (*4. 1, 3, 7; 4. 4-8; 4. 9, 12-15; 5. 1-17; 12. 1-16, 17-20; 24. 15-24; 37. 15-17*).

The prophets were determined by any means to get their message across to men. Here again there is something which is significant. The prophets were entirely willing to experiment. They would never like the modern Church have gone on doing the same things in the same way to an ever-diminishing public. They would have insisted on finding some way to make their message come alive.

Once when Rudyard Kipling was on a world tour, General Booth boarded the ship in New Zealand. He was seen off by a company of hallelujah-shouting and tambourine-beating Salvationists, and Kipling's conventional mind was shocked to the core at this demonstration of religion. Later he met the General and told him what he thought of him. ' Young man,' said the General, ' if I thought I could win one more soul for Christ by standing on my head and beating the tambourine with my feet, I would learn how to do it.' That was the spirit of the prophets—and that is the spirit which has largely been lost in the Church.

To the prophets nature and history were the arena and the sphere of the action of God. The prophets fought their non-stop battle against the worship of the created rather than the Creator and against the creeping pestilence of syncretistic worship. The prophets thundered their insistence that neither liturgy nor ritual, however magnificent, can take the place of conduct and of action, determined by ethical principles. The prophets insisted that religion must be turned into political action and into social justice. The prophets insisted that responsibility is always the other side of privilege, and that, if God chooses a man

25

or a nation, that man or nation is chosen for a task. The prophet saw the world moving, not haphazardly, but towards a goal and a consummation, which was at once a judgment and a remaking of the world. To the prophets the bond between God and his people is the bond between a lover and his beloved. The prophets clothed their message in a magnificence of words, and were prepared to use any method to make men listen.

It is nearly three thousand years ago since they spoke to men, but they are still speaking for him who has ears to hear and a heart to understand.

CHAPTER 2

COMMUNICATING THE GOSPEL
IN THE APOSTLES

WE are left in no doubt at all about the creed of the early Church. That creed was the affirmation, *Jesus Christ is Lord*. It is Paul's dream, and Paul believed that it was God's dream, that a day would come when every tongue would confess that Jesus Christ is Lord (*Philippians 2. 11*). Paul writes to the Romans: ' If you confess with your lips that Jesus Christ is Lord, and believe in your heart that God raised him from the dead, you will be saved ' (*Romans 10. 9*). No one, he says, can say that Jesus Christ is Lord except by the influence of the Holy Spirit (*I Corinthians 12. 3*). It is Peter's injunction to his people: ' In your hearts reverence Christ as Lord ' (*I Peter 3. 15*). So, then, the Christian was first and foremost a man who declared that for him Jesus Christ is Lord. What then exactly did this confession mean?

The word in question is the word *kurios*, and it is an extremely interesting word. Its great value as a credal word was that it has what might be called a ladder of meanings, and it was possible to enter it at any level.

i. *Kurios* is the normal Greek word of respect, equivalent to the English, Sir. It is the word of respect used by the servant to the master, by the younger to the older, by the pupil or the student to his teacher. At its lowest it implies at least respect.

ii. Connected with this is its use in letters. The son writes to his *kurios pater;* it is used as in English we use 'My dear' at the beginning of a letter. It implies at least affection.

iii. It is the normal Greek word for 'owner.' It is, for example, the word for the owner of the vineyard (*Matthew* 21. 40). It is the word which denotes absolute and undisputed possession of anything.

iv. It is the normal Greek word for 'master' as opposed to 'slave.' No man can serve two *kurioi*, two masters (*Matthew* 6. 24). It is the word which denotes absolute authority of one person over another.

v. Closely connected with this last use there are two other related uses. It is the word for the father as the head of the house and home and family. He has the authority; it is his word that goes; it is he who has the final and the indisputable say. Second, it is the regular word for a magistrate or a commander who has the authority to make executive decisions. It describes the person whose word is law.

vi. Before we leave the legal side of this word we have to note another meaning. In Greek law a woman was a thing; she had no legal rights whatsoever. If, then, there was anything which legally affected her, she had to be represented by her guardian, usually her father, or, if her father was dead, often her brother. And the woman's guardian was her *kurios*.

Even if we go no further than this, we can see that *kurios* has the most far-reaching implications when it is applied to Jesus. To call Jesus *kurios* means at the lowest that we give him our respect. It means that we regard ourselves as his absolute possession and him as our absolute and indisputable master. It means that we look on him as the one who has the authority to make the decisions which we are bound to accept. It means that we regard him as the guardian of our lives, to whom we have handed over all our rights. But this word goes further than this.

vii. *Kurios* became the standard title for the Roman Emperor. This use began in the East, where people were naturally more subservient, but it spread to the west, and it became the regular and the standard word in which the imperial might of Rome was summarised.

viii. *Kurios* was the standard title of all the ancient gods and goddesses. It was the title of divinity which was prefixed to all their names in the sense of Lord. Serapis, for instance, was *Kurios Serapis*, the Lord Serapis. *Kurios* was the title which prefixed the name of a god.

ix. *Kurios* has to take its last and final step. When the Old Testament was translated into Greek, in the version known as the Septuagint, *kurios* was the Greek word which was regularly used to translate the Hebrew word *Jahweh*, the name of God himself. *Kurios* at its greatest height means nothing less than God.

So, then, we have to add to the meanings that we have already seen that, if we call Jesus *kurios*, we call him the King and the Emperor of our lives; we call him the Divine One; we call him nothing less than God.

Jesus Christ is Lord is a confession not to be taken lightly on the lips. There are those who speak glibly and easily of ' the Lord Jesus Christ,' but when we remember all that *kurios* means, we shall understand the word of Jesus, when he said, ' Not everyone who says to me, Lord, Lord, shall enter the kingdom of heaven, but he who does the will of my Father who is in heaven ' (*Matthew 7. 21*).

That Jesus Christ is Lord was the proclamation of the early Church, and we can see that this word Lord is nothing less than a whole theology in one word.

Before we look at the general content of the apostolic message there are two points of method which we must notice. We are well supplied with material from which we can reconstruct both the content and the method of the apostolic preaching. We have Peter's sermon in Jerusalem in *Acts 2*; we have Paul's three sermons, the first in Antioch in Pisidia in *Acts 13*, the second in Lystra in *Acts 14*, and the third in Athens in *Acts 17*. The interesting and the important fact is that, when we look at the three Pauline sermons, they are totally different. And they are different because each of them is specially and particularly designed for the audience to which it was addressed. As a preacher Paul had an amazing gift for starting from where his audience was. His basic message is the same, but he had an astonishing gift of technique which enabled him to adapt that message to the audience which he was addressing.

In Antioch in Pisidia he was addressing Jews in a Jewish Synagogue, and the only Gentiles present would be either full proselytes or at least God-fearers who were interested in Judaism. When Paul spoke to this audience, he began in the Old Testament; he continued in the Old Testament; and he ended in the life of Jesus as fulfilment of the Old Testament. He knew that to his audience the Old Testament was sacred and holy Scripture, and he knew that they both knew it and accepted its authority ; so he therefore made it the basis of what he had to say.

In Athens, Paul's method was quite different. There he was not speaking in a Jewish Synagogue but in the open air. He was not speaking to a Jewish audience, but to a Greek audience. He therefore began with quotations from the Greek poets and philosophers. Paul was well aware that there is no good in saying, ' The Bible says,' to a man who neither knows nor accepts the Bible. The wise preacher begins where his audience is and with what they know to lead them on to where he wants them to be and what he wants them to learn. So, as Paul was a Jew to the Jews, to the Greek he became a Greek.

In Lystra once again Paul's method was quite different. In Lystra he was out in the wilds. There was no Synagogue there and there was no Greek culture there. It would have been futile to quote the Old Testament and it would have been equally pointless to quote the Greek poets and philosophers; so there Paul starts from the sun and the wind and the rain and from growing things—things which all men know.

Here is a great lesson for the preacher. Dr. Johnson was one of the greatest and the wisest talkers the world has ever seen. Mrs. Thrale was one of his close friends and benefactors. Mrs. Thrale had a young friend who did brilliantly at his university and then perforce became the vicar of a country parish. He was quite sure that his intellectual gifts were wasted on these barbaric and bucolic countrymen, most of whom were farmers and ploughmen and cattlemen. ' All that they can talk about,' he said contemptuously to Mrs. Thrale, ' is runts.' (Runts are young cattle.) ' Sir,' said Mrs. Thrale, ' if Dr. Johnson had been the parson of your parish, he would have learned to talk about runts.' The true preacher starts where his people are—even if he has to learn about things he never in his life heard about before. The sermon which is above a congregation's heads is not a good sermon; it is a bad sermon. It is simply the sign of a marksman who cannot hit the target. Be it noted that the preacher does not wish to *leave* his people where they are—far from that. But he begins from where they are to lead them to where he would wish them to be.

The second notable thing was something which emerged from the pattern of the Synagogue service. The brief outline of the Synagogue service was this.

i. It began with the *Shema*, which is the basic Jewish creed. *Shema* is the imperative of the Hebrew verb *to hear*, and means ' Hear!' It is the first word of that verse which is the fundamental creed of Judaism, ' Hear, O Israel; the Lord our God is one Lord ' (*Deuteronomy 6. 4*). Before the *Shema* there came one set prayer and after it one or two prayers. Following the *Shema* there came the Eighteen Benedictions, eighteen prayers which bless God for his goodness and his graciousness. Inset into this there is the time for free and for topical prayers which bring the need of the immediate moment to God. This first worship part of the service finishes with the blessing, ' The Lord bless you and keep you; the Lord make his face to shine upon

you, and be gracious to you; the Lord lift up his coun-
tenance upon you, and give you peace ' (*Numbers* 6. 25, 26).

ii. The second part of the service consisted of the
reading of Scripture, one lesson from the Law, and one
from the Prophets. The Law was read from a lectionary,
in which it was read completely through in three years;
the prophetic lesson was chosen by the reader. The lesson
from the Law was read one verse at a time, and, since by
New Testament times the Jews had forgotten their
classical Hebrew, it was translated by an official called
the Targumist, also one verse at a time. The lesson from
the prophets was read and translated in the same way,
but three verses at a time.

iii. Lastly, there came the preaching, which was
always in the nature of the exposition of Scripture.

Such was the outline of the service, but simply to
state the outline is omit the most significant thing about
the whole service. The most significant thing is that there
was no one officially to do any of these things, with the
single exception of the blessing which was always pro-
nounced by a priest, if there was a priest present. There
was no professional ministry at all. There was an official
known as the Ruler, or the Head, of the Synagogue but he
was purely an administrative official. He had to do with
the finance and the organisation and the care of the
buildings; and he had to do with the service to the extent
that a chairman or president has to do with a meeting.
He did not himself do any of the items; he saw that they
were correctly done. What then happened?

Everything in the service was done by members of

the congregation. A man called the Ambassador of the Congregation was detailed to take the prayer part of the service; seven people, a priest, a Levite, (if present), and five ordinary members of the congregation, from the congregation were called up to read the passage from the Law, so many verses each; one man was told to choose and read the lesson from the prophets. Anyone who felt he had an address to give could give it. It was precisely here that in the early days the Christian preachers got their chance; it was here that Paul got his chance. Under modern conditions they would never have been allowed to utter a word. But in the Synagogue, when it came time for the sermon, anyone who had a message to give could, subject to the approval of the Head of the Synagogue, give it. And until the breach between the Church and the Synagogue was final, here was a magnificent chance which the Christian preachers seized with both hands.

But we have still not come to the most important feature of the service for the communication of the Christian message. The sermon was always followed by general discussion, and it was exactly here that the Christian preacher got the greatest chance of all to communicate the Christian message. The word that we come on again and again in regard to the preaching of the Christian preachers in the Synagogue is the word *dispute* or *argue*. The Jews disputed with Stephen but could not meet his arguments (*Acts*, 6. 9, 10). Paul argued in the Synagogue at Thessalonica (*Acts* 17. 2); he argued in the Synagogue at Corinth (*Acts* 18. 2); he argued in the Synagogue at Ephesus (*Acts* 18. 19). Here is the great basic fact of early preaching. *Early preaching was not a monologue but a dialogue.* It was not a question of one man telling a crowd of men; it was a case of a group of people talking it over together. Of course, there should be services of worship and certainty in which the atmosphere of debate would be out of place; but there ought also to be a place for the contact of mind with mind. For, if there is not, how is the preacher to know that he is asking and answering the right questions at all? If he does not give to those to whom he speaks an opportunity to speak to him, then he may be completely missing their problems, and he may be quite unaware of their doubts and difficulties. We shall always need the monologue, but the rediscovery of the dialogue within the Church is long overdue. It was just that dialogue which gave the apostolic preachers their supreme opportunity. It could still be so today.

Let us now turn directly to the message which the early apostolic Church did deliver to men. When we examine the sermons in the Book of Acts, we find that they have a pattern. There are certain recurring strands in them. All the strands do not occur in all the sermons, but when they are all put together they do give the pattern of the message of the early Church. To this essential message a name has been given. It has been called the *kerugma*. *Kerugma* means *a herald's announcement*, and the *kerugma* is the basic message of the apostolic preaching.

i. The first announcement of the *kerugma* is, The new age has dawned, and it has dawned through the life, the death and the resurrection of Jesus Christ.

When we were studying the prophets we saw that

one of their basic conceptions is that all time is divided into two ages; there is this present age which is under the domination of the devil and of evil, and which is power-less to save itself. There is the age which is to come, the new age, which is the age of God and his kingdom; and we also saw that the prophets expected the one age to turn into the other, not by any effort of man, but by the direct intervention of God. The message of the apostolic preaching is that God has acted in Jesus Christ, and that the new age has come. In Jesus something new has hap-pened and that something new is the work of God. With Jesus Christ there came into the world something new. Now it so happens that this is factually and historically demonstrable. It is demonstrable in four areas of life.

(a) In Jesus Christ something new happened for the child. In the ancient world life was dangerous for the child. When a child was born he was laid at his father's feet. If the father stooped and picked up the child, the child was kept; if the father turned and walked away, the child was quite literally thrown out.

There was no law against this; it was perfectly legal. There was no stigma attaching to it; it was the accepted custom. There is a famous letter dating from 1 A.D. from a man Hilarion, who at the time of writing was away from home, to his wife Alis. He writes, ' I know you are expecting a child. If it is a boy keep it, if it is a girl throw it out.' This was the perfectly recognised and accepted custom.

There was never a night when there were not forty or fifty abandoned babies in the forum at Rome. They were collected by those who had made it a business to do so.

The fortunate were sold to women who wanted a child without the trouble of having one of their own. More often, the boys were kept and trained up to be gladiators to fight in the arena, and the girls were trained up to stock the brothels of Rome. So common was this that one of the early Christian apologists warned Roman men that, when they frequented brothels, they could never be sure that it was not their own daughters they were using. Some were sold to beggars who deliberately mutilated them, and then took them with them when they begged, to awaken the sympathy of the passers-by. Girl babies were thrown out much oftener than boys, for girls were only a useless expense, whereas the boys could be profitable as wage-earners. If a child was in any way weak or sickly, his chances of survival were small. Plato laid it down that in his ideal Republic no such child should be allowed to live. And this was not merely a philosopher's dream, for Seneca says, ' We strangle a fierce ox; we kill a mad dog; we plunge the knife into sickly cattle lest they taint the herd; children who are born weakly or deformed we drown.' It was the accepted custom.

These things cannot happen nowadays in any society which has been touched by the principles of Jesus Christ. It is not that society is fully Christian, but with the coming of Jesus Christ something happened that made things like that impossible. With the coming of Jesus Christ something happened for the child.

(b) In Jesus Christ something new happened for women. It is true that within the home there can never have been a time when the mother did not reign supreme.

37

D

But in the eyes of both Jewish and Roman law a woman was a thing; she had no legal rights whatsoever. To educate a woman was to cast pearls before swine, so women were entirely uneducated. In law, for instance, a woman could not divorce her husband, while all that the husband had to do was to tell the woman to go.

In the East, still untouched by Christian principles, Bernard Newman tells how he once saw a man make his wife walk in front of a camel through a piece of ground during the war time in which there was a possibility that there might be unexploded mines. His excuse, for him his reason, for doing this was that the camel was valuable, and he did not want it to run the risk of injury.

It is the simple fact that it was with Christ that chivalry was born.

(c) In Jesus Christ something happened for the working man. Again it is a fact of history that no one owes more to Jesus Christ than the working man. The Roman Empire was built on slavery; in it there were 60,000,000 slaves, and every one of these slaves was classified as a thing; they were defined as living tools. A master had absolute power over his slave. He could lash him, he could starve him, he could put him in chains, he could kill him; it was all perfectly legal.

One of the Roman writers on agriculture gives advice to a farmer taking over a new farm. Throw out the old spades and hoes and farm implements; clear them out, if they are past their usefulness. And throw out any old slaves who are past their work. They will starve and die? What does it matter? They are merely things, of no more importance than the implements and the cattle of the farm.

Once again, we cannot imagine that happening now. Why? Because in Jesus Christ something happened for the working-man; and if ever the principles of Jesus Christ go lost or are forgotten, the old tyrannies will come back, for that which gives any man his value is nothing other than the Christian belief that he matters to God.

(d) Above all, in Jesus Christ something happened for the sinner. It was not that that ancient world did not know its sin; it knew it all right; and it hated it all right; but it could not leave it. Persius told the rich debauchee, ' Look on virtue, and pine that you have lost her for ever.' There never was a world so conscious both of its sin and of its own helplessness.

It was just here that Christianity came in offering the victory—and to this we will return. There is that amazing passage in *I Corinthians 6. 9-11,*

' Do you not know that the unrighteous will not inherit the kingdom of God? Do not be deceived; neither the immoral, nor idolaters, nor adulterers, nor homosexuals, nor thieves, nor the greedy, nor drunkards, nor revilers, nor robbers, will inherit the kingdom of God.'

And then, after the dreadful list, there comes the shout of sheer triumph,

' And such were some of you. But you were washed, your were sanctified, you were justified in the name of the Lord Jesus Christ and in the Spirit of our God.'

In Jesus Christ something triumphantly happened for the sinner.

ii. The second item in the *kerugma* was, all this is the direct fulfilment of prophecy. The life, the death, the resurrection of Jesus Christ, all that he was and did, all that happened to him, are the direct fulfilment of prophecy.

In regard to this, two things emerge. The first is something which, if we are going to be honest, we must face. It is the simple fact that we cannot use prophecy as the New Testament writers used it. The New Testament writers were, in the interpretation of Scripture, children of their age. They annexed any Old Testament passage which could be verbally used to prove their point. Out of many instances of this we take but one. Matthew says that the flight into Egypt of Mary and Joseph and the child Jesus fulfils the prophecy of Hosea (*11. 1*), ' Out of Egypt have I called my son.' But what happens when we look up Hosea? Here is the Hosea passage:

' When Israel was a child, I loved him,
  and out of Egypt I called my son.
The more I called them, the more they went from me,
  they kept sacrificing to the Baals,
  and burning incense to idols.'

In Hosea the passage is not a prophecy at all; it is a statement of something which happened; it tells how under Moses at the exodus God called his people Israel out of the land of Egypt. And yet Matthew uses this as a prophecy of the Flight into Egypt of Jesus and his family—something with which it has nothing at all to do.

To understand this we must understand the Jewish way of interpreting scripture. For a Jew every passage of

Scripture had four meanings. First, it had the meaning called *Peshat*, which is the simple meaning, the meaning that lies on the surface. Second, it had the meaning called *Remaz*, which means the suggested meaning. Third, it had the meaning called *Derush*, which is the meaning after investigation, after all the resources and tools of scholarship have been brought to bear upon the passage. Last, it has the meaning called *Sod*. *Sod* is the spiritual, the allegorical meaning, the meaning which can be read into the passage, and for the Jew that was the most important meaning of all. Now this meant that the Jew could pretty well make scripture mean anything that he wanted it to mean; and he could seize on merely verbal connections which are not really connections at all.

If we are honest, we can no longer do this. Many of the arguments from prophecy will no longer be at all convincing to us. But this does not mean that the argument from prophecy no longer means anything at all.

Behind the argument from prophecy there lies a principle of the first importance. If it is possible to speak of prophecy at all, it means that there is a purpose and a plan in history. If it is possible to point to some goal or consummation which is going to happen, it means that history is going somewhere. It means, to put it at its widest, that history is the arena of the action of God.

It is far from everyone who has been able to believe this. Amongst the ancient Greeks, the Stoics believed that history is circular. They believed that every so often the world went up in a cosmic conflagration; and then, they believed, the whole process started all over again in exactly and precisely the same way, and to the last detail ever kept happening over and over again—with the merciful proviso that we do not remember our previous existences. This theory means that history is a treadmill for ever going round and round and getting no further on.

In modern times there has been a pessimism about history. In his inaugural lecture at Cambridge, G. N. Clark said, ' There is no secret and no plan in history to be discovered. I do not believe that any future consummation could make sense of all the irrationalities of preceding ages. If it could not explain them, still less could it justify them.' H. A. L. Fisher, the famous author of *The History of Europe*, wrote, ' One intellectual excitement, however, has been denied to me. Men wiser and more learned than I have discovered in history a plot, a rhythm, a predetermined pattern. These harmonies are concealed from me. I can see only one emergency following upon another as wave follows upon wave . . . nothing but the play of the contingent and the unforeseeable.' André Maurois wrote, ' The universe is indifferent. Who created it? Why are we here on this puny mudheap spinning in infinite space? I have not the slightest idea, and I am quite convinced that no one has the least idea.'

Gerald Healy, in his play *The Black Stranger*, describes the events of the tragic Irish potato famine in 1846. Men had been set digging roads which had no beginning and no end and no purpose. They were simply set digging as an excuse for giving them some kind of pay. Michael, the son, suddenly discovers what is happening, and he comes home and says, sad and bewildered, 'They're makin' roads that lead to nowhere.'

The views that we have been quoting see history as a road that leads to nowhere. There are times when such a view is intolerable. If we are called on to suffer and to sacrifice, as any generation may be, then, if all this is to some purpose, it is bearable and tolerable, but if the whole thing is utterly senseless, then life is tragedy.

The very fact that the early preachers used the idea of prophecy is the sign that it is the Christian conviction, to which we must always hold, that history is not a haphazard progress to nowhere; it is the unfolding of the purpose and the plan of God.

iii. The third item in the apostolic announcement was the declaration that Jesus Christ has ascended to the right hand of God and that he would come again to judge the quick and the dead. There is no doctrine of the Christian faith which so much needs restatement and rethinking as does the doctrine of the Second Coming. There are many Churches in which it is never heard of at all, and in which it is looked on as one of the eccentricities of the Christian faith. There are preachers who can think of little else, and for whom it is by far the most important doctrine of the Christian faith.

We shall have to begin by recognizing that the doctrine of the Second Coming is stated in the New Testament in terms of the New Testament's time. It is just no longer possible for us to think in terms of Jesus coming down on the clouds. We cannot any longer think of heaven as merely somewhere 'up.' If that were so, if it could be propelled far enough, a space rocket or vessel might ultimately reach heaven. The old 'up' and 'down' language, which was easy and natural for a first century man, is no longer possible. But nonetheless this was an essential part of the early preaching, so let us see if we can state it in terms of today.

There are three possible ways of thinking of the Second Coming.

i. We can think of it as an event in the future, which will happen suddenly, startlingly and shatteringly. If we do think of it in that way, then we have no right at all to speculate when it will happen, for Jesus himself said that the day and the hour were unknown to him (*Mark* 13. 32). It is not within the bounds of possibility for a Christian to draw up celestial time-tables like that.

ii. It is possible to hold, and many Christians in all ages have held, that the Second Coming happened at Pentecost, that then Jesus came powerfully in the Spirit, never again to be separated from his own.

iii. But there is a third view for which there is evidence in the New Testament itself. A certain characteristic difference between the eastern and the western mind has been pointed out. The eastern mind tends to think in flashpoints; it tends to picture things as happening suddenly in a flash and in a split second of time. On the other hand, the western mind, with its greater knowledge of the universe and its laws, tends to think of things as happening rather through a process than at a flashpoint.

Let us take two examples of this. The Hebrew mind

thinks of *creation* as happening in a flashpoint, all over in a week. The western mind tends to think of creation as a long process under the control of God, taking centuries to work out. In both cases God is the creator, but in one case he creates in a flashpoint, in the other he creates as a process in which his purposes slowly throughout the ages unfold; in the one case it is something which is over and done with, in the other it is a continuing action of God in and upon the world.

The second example is *judgment.* There are parts of the New Testament in which judgment is set out and depicted as a future event; but there are other parts of the Bible in which judgment is a continuing process. In the Fourth Gospel, judgment is something which is not deferred to some distant future but which is going on all the time. In the Fourth Gospel, judgment happens every time a man is confronted with Christ. In that moment, by his response to Jesus Christ, he is already judged. According to John (*John 5. 24*) Jesus said, ' Truly, truly I say to you, he who hears my word and believes him who sent me, has eternal life; he does not come into judgment, but has passed from death to life.'

This means that judgment is not a future event, but something which is going on all the time, as a continuous process, every time a man is confronted with Jesus Christ.

Now John has also something to say which is very significant for the Second Coming. Jesus said (*John 14. 23*), ' If a man loves me, he will keep my word; and my Father will love him; *and we will come to him and make our home with him.*' This is to say, Jesus says that he and his Father come to the man who loves and trusts God.

There is a very strong case for looking at the Second Coming in two ways, for looking at it personally and cosmically. I think that we might well say that for a man personally the Second Coming happens whenever he is converted, and when Jesus Christ comes into his heart, and I think that we might also say that the Second Coming stands for the ultimate triumph of Jesus, the event to which all creation moves, the day when Jesus Christ is Lord for all the earth.

iv. The fourth item in the apostolic preaching is an invitation and a promise. It is an invitation in view of all this to repent, and to receive the gift of the Holy Spirit.

It is important to see just what is being demanded and just what is being promised.

There is nothing more important for the Christian life than to establish the correct meaning of the word *repentance.* We might say at first sight that repentance means being sorry for the wrong things that we have done. But there is one thing clearly to be seen. Repentance does not mean simply being sorry for the consequences of what we have done; for a man might be sorry for the consequences, and might be ready and willing and even eager to do the same thing again, if he thought that he could escape the consequences. In Greek, repentance is *metanoia,* and *metanoia* literally means *a change of mind.* It means, not simply that we are sorry for the consequences of what we have done, although often the consequences are the way to the realisation of the evil of the thing—it

46

means that we have a changed attitude to the whole thing. It means that we have seen something that makes us sorry that we ever were as we were and did as we did. It is a kind of self-loathing in face of the revelation in Christ of what life ought to be. Repentance is a changed attitude to life in which we are not only sorry for the consequences of what we have done, but in which we hate the sin that made us do it.

With this demand there comes an offer. It is the offer of the forgiveness of sins and of the gift of the Holy Spirit. The offer of the first preaching was twofold. It was forgiveness for the past, and it was the gift of the Holy Spirit for the future. It was release from the past and strength for the future.

It must always be noted that the early preaching was not only concerned with a man's past; it was equally concerned with his future. It offered him forgiveness for what he had done and the strength not to do it again.

v. There was one last item in the apostolic preaching and it is the obverse of the promise. The early preaching offered a promise, but, if the promise was rejected, it ended with a threat.

From beginning to end, the Bible is always saying, ' Choose ye!' It has been said, and said truly, that Christianity concentrates upon man at the cross roads. It offered life, but it had no doubt that, if the life was refused, the end was death.

It is the same voice as Bunyan heard on the village green at Bedford, ' Wilt thou have thy sins and go to hell, or wilt thou leave thy sins and go to heaven?'

The greatest offer in the world can only be turned down at the greatest peril in the world.

This, then, was the gospel which the apostolic preaching proclaimed. The new age has dawned; God has acted directly in the life and the death and the Resurrection of Jesus Christ. All this is the fulfilment of prophecy and the very conception of prophecy implies a plan and a purpose which are being steadily worked out in the world. This Jesus who lived and died and rose again will come again; he will come to the individual heart, and in the end he will triumph over all the world. There comes the demand for repentance, for a new attitude to life and to living, and the promise of forgiveness for the past and strength for the future. And finally there comes the threat that, if a man will not accept life, then he has accepted death.

CHAPTER 3

COMMUNICATING THE GOSPEL TODAY

I TAKE IT that all here will be agreed that the task of the
Christian Church in this, as in any other, age is to communicate to men the truth of God as we find it in the word
of God. How then can we best communicate the word of
God to men? What will be our approach to the Bible
when we try to fulfil our task of opening its truth to men?

It is possible to make a large number of different
approaches to any book. It is possible, for instance, to make
many approaches to Shakespeare's play *Julius Caesar*.

Here is a boy reading it that he may pass his Advanced
Level Leaving Certificate in English on it. Here is a University student reading it in a much more detailed way that
he may pass his degree examination on it. Here is the
student of Roman history reading it to see what light it
will throw upon his subject. Here is the Shakespearean
specialist reading it to see what light it casts upon Shakespeare's methods as a dramatist. Here is a student of blank
verse reading it to analyse the way in which Shakespeare
writes his poetry. Here is the textual critic reading it in
a search for places where the text is to be corrected or
emended. Here is the student of psychology reading it to
make a study of the psychology of Cassius. Here is the
student of literature and poetry reading it to extend and
expand his knowledge of that subject. And last—and by
no means least—here is a man reading it for no other
reason than that he enjoys reading it. It is then possible

to make a wide variety of approaches to any book. What, then, are the approaches we must make to the New Testament to communicate it to men today?

i. First and foremost, to begin at the beginning, we must approach it as *literature*. It is the fact that anyone who has not read the Bible is simply from the literary point of view not properly educated. It was Coleridge's advice as a writer that any writer ought to read the Bible, because, he said, constant study of the Bible will keep any man from being vulgar in point of style.

In his chapter on the English Bible in his book *The Englishman*, McNeile Dixon points out how ' the golden stream of language ' which flows from the Bible is inextricably interwoven into the English language. He points out how again and again writers and speakers quote the Bible, not in quotation marks, but quite unconsciously and automatically. He quotes the example of an American professor who made a note of the quotations from, and references and allusions to, the Bible, made simply as a part of the general language, in three books that he happened to be reading. One was on an Italian subject, one was on the life of wild animals, and one was a novel of Thomas Hardy's. In the first there were 63 quotations; in the second 12; and in the third 18.

Here is a passage which might have occurred in the sports edition of any Saturday evening newspaper,

' It seems as *clear as crystal* that, unless changes are made *at the eleventh hour*, the Scottish team to play England must *lick the dust*. At best they can only hope to escape *by the skin of their teeth*. Too many of the team have been *weighed in the balance and found wanting*. Certain of the players are by this time but *broken reeds*, and some of them for too long have been *a law unto themselves*, and *a thorn in the flesh* both to the captain and to the team manager. They badly need *a word in season*, or their *talents may well be wasted*. It may be that the selectors might be well advised to go out into the *highways and hedges* to seek new players. We sadly fear that for Scotland in the international arena *the glory is departed*.'

In that paragraph there are no fewer than twelve quotations from the Bible, and to them we might add such well known phrases as a labour of love, hip and thigh, the shadow of death, coals of fire, a soft answer. The language of this book is interwoven into the English language.

The need for this approach is specially strong today, because of the ignorance of the Bible. John Masefield told how he once received a letter from a University graduate saying, ' I have just come across what I think is a very beautiful quotation. I wonder if you could tell me from what book it comes, and where I could get a copy. The quotation is, "Blessed are the pure in heart for they shall see God".' Early in the war Captain Liddell Hart, the famous expert in military strategy, used a biblical phrase to express himself. Liddell Hart was opposed to conscription and he said, ' What this country wants is a Gideon army.' Most people had no idea what he meant. The reference is in *Judges* 7. 1-7. When Gideon sent out the fiery cross, 32,000 men responded. God told Gideon that that was far too many, so those who were afraid were told to go home, and 22,000 went home. 10,000 remained, and these were still too many. So God told Gideon to take them down to the water and to tell them to drink. Those who knelt down and drank by plunging their heads almost into the water were set on one side; and those who drank by lifting the water to their mouths in their hands were set on the other side. Those who knelt down to drink were 9700, and they were told to go home, doubtless because they drank without keeping watch. Those who lapped the water with their hands were 300 and they were the chosen band. Such was a Gideon army, and for Liddell Hart's purposes it was a vivid and effective picture—but there were few who recognized it.

If the Bible is to be read as literature, certain things become necessary.

(a) We must get into the habit of reading the Bible in long sections. We far too often get into the habit, perhaps unconsciously, of looking on the Bible as a book from which ten or twenty verses are taken as a reading lesson, from which a dozen verses are taken to be the subject of a lesson or of a Bible study, from which a preacher takes a single verse on which to preach a sermon. This is to say we regard the Bible as a book on which we turn the microscope. For that reason we never see the sweep, the drama, the panorama of the story.

You would never take a novel and sit down and read one page this week and then lay it down until next week before you read the next page. You read it sometimes at a sitting. Take the Gospel of Mark and read it right through at a sitting, and see the drama of the life of Jesus—

preparation, conflict, tragedy, triumph, emerging like a four act thrilling play.

It would be well if we would stop treating the Bible as a book of lessons and problems, and read it simply as a book with the most moving and thrilling story on earth to tell.

(b) It will greatly help to get a properly printed and translated Bible. No book suffers more in the printing than the Bible does. In the normal printing of the Authorised Version there are certain words in italic print. Normally italic print is the sign of a word that is stressed or specially important; in the Authorised Version italic print is the sign of a word for which there is no equivalent in the Hebrew or the Greek and which has had to be inserted to fill out the meaning.

The Bible as we have it is divided into chapters and verses. This is useful and even essential for reference; but this was no part of the original. The chapter divisions were put in by Stephen Langton in the 13th century; and the verse divisions were first put in by the Paris printer, Stephanus, in the 17th century; he actually put them in when he was day by day riding on horseback between his house and his printing works—and someone has said that it looks like it.

(c) It will help even more to get a properly translated Bible. The Authorised Version is one of the supreme monuments of the English language. What, then, is wrong with it, and why should we wish to abandon it? There are two things wrong with it.

1. There is nothing so much wrong with the trans-

53

lation of the Old Testament, because the Old Testament is written in the most beautiful classical Hebrew, which only the most beautiful English is adequate to translate. But the whole point of the New Testament is that it is written in the most colloquial, everyday Greek, Greek which is often ungrammatical, Greek which quite commonly uses slang words, Greek which the ordinary men and women spoke to each other every day. It is in fact true that, even if you completely disregard the religious value of the New Testament, its linguistic value is incalculable, for it is the one surviving bit of Greek literature written in the language which people spoke every day.

The Authorised Version is far too beautiful; the English is far too lovely; it gives precisely the wrong effect nowadays; the Greek of the New Testament is the short, snappy, colloquial kind of language that you read in your daily newspaper. Further, the Authorised Version is in Elizabethan English with its ' thou's ' and its ' thee's ' and all the rest of it, the whole atmosphere is archaic; and when it was written its whole atmosphere was completely contemporary. If only we would realise that we do not read the Bible for the beauty of its language; there is no point in luxuriating in the beauty of it; there is no point in being so charmed with how it sounds that we forget what it says. To see how the New Testament ought to sound we must read it in the kind of language that we speak every day.

2. But there is something more serious than that. The foundation of the New Testament is, of course, the

ancient Greek manuscripts. Now these manuscripts were, of course, written long before the age of printing; they were copied by hand. Now everyone knows that it is an inevitable fact that every time a thing is copied new mistakes creep in. Human fallibility is such that this is unavoidable. This will mean that the older a manuscript is the more likely it is to be correct. It will have been copied far fewer times and it will be nearer the original writing.

Now the Authorised Version was made in 1611, and it was mainly dependent on the Greek text published by Erasmus between 1520 and 1530. Erasmus' Greek text is almost entirely dependent on two Greek manuscripts which date to the 9th and 10th centuries, that is to say, 900 years away from the original writing. Erasmus was not to blame for this; it was all that was available to him; the great Greek manuscripts had not yet been brought to light and discovered.

Today we possess manuscripts which go back to the middle of the 3rd century; and the great manuscripts are 4th and 5th century. That is to say, today we have manuscripts which are more than 600 years older than the manuscripts on which the Authorised Version is founded. Further, we today have at least 2000 uncial and 8000 minuscule manuscripts to use. We have almost 10,000 manuscripts which in the day of Erasmus were undiscovered and unknown. That is why, for all its supreme beauty, the Authorised Version is not a satisfactory translation of the New Testament, and that is why, if we really want to study the Bible and see what it is really saying, we need a modern translation. That is why I am convinced that it is time that we stopped regarding the Authorised Version as if it was the word of God, and took to using all the time one of the newer translations like the Revised Standard Version or the New English Bible.

So then the first approach to the New Testament must be the approach to it as literature.

ii. The second approach to the New Testament must be the *linguistic* approach. This is obvious, for, if we regard the Bible as the supreme rule of faith and life, then clearly the very first necessity is to be quite sure what it is saying. Therefore, one of the essential approaches to the New Testament is the study of the meaning of its words. Let us take certain examples of just how illuminating this kind of approach can be.

In the Authorised Version, the Beatitude runs, 'Blessed are the meek, for they shall inherit the earth' (*Matthew* 5. 5). The word *meek* is not now a good word. It tends to describe someone who is spiritless and spineless and who would not say ' boo ' to a goose. It would not really attract vivid and virile six-formers to tell them that the Christian ethic insists that they must be meek.

Let us, then, look at this word. In Greek, it is the word *praotes*, which is the noun, and *praus*, which is the adjective. Aristotle, the greatest of the Greek ethical writers, has a long discussion of the meaning of *praotes*. For Aristotle every virtue was the mean between two extremes, between the extreme of excess on one side and defect on the other. So on the one hand you have the reckless man and on the other hand you have the coward, and in between you have the mean, the happy medium, of the brave man. On the one hand you have the miser, and on the other hand you have the spendthrift, and in between, in the mean, you have the properly generous man. Aristotle takes this word *praotes* and he defines it as the mean in regard to anger, and he says that it describes the mean, the happy medium, between excessive anger and excessive angerlessness. He then describes the man who is *praus* as the man who is angry for the right reasons, against the right people, in the right way, and for the right length of time. You may therefore translate, 'Blessed are the meek,' as, ' Happy is the man who is always angry at the right time and never angry at the wrong time '—and that, indeed, means something.

Let us take a Pauline phrase. Three times Paul speaks of what he calls the *earnest* of the Spirit (*2 Corinthians 1. 22; 5. 5; Ephesians 1. 14*). To modern ears this phrase has very little meaning. In Greek the word is *arrabon*. *Arrabon* is a very common business word in contracts and in agreements Its regular meaning is *an advance payment in part, as a guarantee that the full price will in due time be paid*. Let us see just how widely this word is used in secular business and commercial Greek. A woman sells a cow, and she receives so much as *arrabon*, the first instalment of the price, and the guarantee that the full price will be paid. A man is engaged as a mouse-catcher in a vineyard. He is at once paid so much as *arrabon* so that he can begin immediately on the job. An Egyptian village is having a celebration and its officials engage a troup of castanet dancing-girls, and they are paid so much as *arrabon*, when the agreement is made as a guarantee that, when they have duly performed, the full price will be paid.

So then this word *arrabon* means both a first instalment and a guarantee that the full final price will in the end be paid. When Paul speaks of the earnest of the Spirit, he means that the gift of the Holy Spirit is the first instalment of the life of heaven, and the guarantee that into the fulness of that heavenly life we shall one day enter.

Let us take still another word, this time an Aramaic word, the word by which Jesus called God in the Garden of Gethsamane, as Mark tells the story. Jesus began his prayer, *Abba*, ' Father ' (*Mark 14. 36*). In many ways this is the most wonderful saying in the New Testament. *Abba* is the word by which a little Jewish child addressed his father in the home. To this day you may hear the little Jewish boy or girl shouting, ' Abba!', through the house. If you came on *Abba* in any Jewish writing, the ordinary and inevitable translation would be, ' Daddy.' It is by that name that we, too, can address God as Paul twice says. We, too, can say to God, ' Abba, Father ' (*Galatians 4. 6; Romans 8. 15*). As Jeremias has pointed out, no one in all history ever spoke to God like that before Jesus Christ. There is no word in the whole Bible which makes so vividly and tenderly clear the new relationship between man and God made possible by Jesus Christ.

Let us take one last word. In the Fourth Gospel we read again and again in the Authorised Version of the Holy Spirit, the *Comforter*. There are few words which have done so much to damage and to limit the doctrine of the Holy Spirit. Nowadays the word *comforter* has only one meaning. It means someone who in sorrow sympathises with us and wipes our tears away. No doubt that is great but it is a very serious limitation of what this word really means. The word is *parakletos*, which has come into English almost exactly as it is in Greek in the word *paraclete*, as in the hymn, ' Come, thou holy Paraclete.' In Greek the word *parakletos* literally means *some who is called in*. It is used for some who is called in to give counsel and advice. It means some one who is called in to give help and healing. It means some one who is called in as a witness for the defence. In Polybius it is used of an orator who is called in to speak to a body of depressed, discouraged and dispirited troops, and who speaks to them with such force and power that the spirit and the courage come back to their hearts, and they become once again a first-class body of fighting men.

All these things *Parakletos* means; it means, not just some one who comforts in sorrow, but some one who gives us strength and power and courage and wisdom to cope with life.

How, then, did the word *Comforter*, now so narrow a word, ever get into the Authorised Version? It was the translation which Wicliffe used in 1386 and it has stayed in the English Bible ever since; but in Wicliffe it was never meant to mean anything so narrow as ' Comforter ' in the modern sense of the term. In 1386 this is not what comforter meant. The word *comforter* is derived from the Latin word *fortis*, and a comforter at that time was some one who filled you with courage, some one who made you brave, some one who made you able to meet the chances and the changes of life erect and unafraid. The Holy Spirit is the great Encourager of men.

It is easy to see what a flood of light the real meaning of the word *parakletos* sheds on the doctrine of the Holy Spirit. That which is already precious acquires a new and and even greater preciousness.

iii. The third approach which is necessary to communicate the New Testament is the *historical* approach. Everything happens against a background in history, and to know that background often adds very greatly to the meaning of the incident. Such a knowledge often brings an incident or a story to life. This is true not only of the stories of the Bible but in any sphere.

There is a story of how Beethoven composed the famous Moonlight Sonata. Late one night, so it is told, Beethoven was coming home through the streets of Bonn. As he passed a house he heard one of his own compositions being played. He went through the garden of the house up to the casement windows and looked in. A girl was sitting at the piano playing, and, as he watched her, Beethoven realised that the girl was blind. He stepped in through the window. ' Let me play that piece of music for you,' he said. In spite of her surprise the girl allowed him to play. He played it so beautifully that the girl said: ' I can only think that you must be Beethoven himself.' ' I am,' he said. For a long time he played to her; it grew dark but to the blind girl the darkness made no difference. At last Beethoven rose to go. The girl said, ' Play me just one more piece before you go.' By this time it was dark with a full moon. Beethoven sat down at the piano which was near the great windows. And the moonlight came slanting across the keys. 'Listen,' said Beethoven, ' and I will play you the moonlight.' And there and then he composed and played the first rippling movement of what is perhaps the most famous sonata in the world. Next time you hear the Moonlight Sonata you will think of that, and that wonderful music will become more wonderful.

Now this is what happens with the New Testament and its stories. Let us take certain examples and illustrations of this.

In *John* 7. 37, we read, ' On the last day of the feast, the great day, Jesus stood up and proclaimed, If anyone thirst let him come to me and drink.' And at the beginning of the next chapter (8. 12) he said, ' I am the light of the world; he who follows me will not walk in darkness, but will have the light of life.' The Festival in question was the Feast of Tabernacles. The main memory of the Feast of Tabernacles was the time of the journey through the wilderness. All through the week the Jews went out of their houses and lived in little tents or booths or tabernacles—hence the name of the festival—and so remembered and commemorated the days when they had travelled in the wilderness and had lived in tents, with no settled home.

On the last day of that festival there were two famous ceremonies. In the first, in the morning the High Priest took a silver pitcher holding two pints of water. He took it from the Temple and he went in procession through the crowds down to the Pool of Siloam and filled it. He began the journey back to the Temple while the crowds in the streets shouted the words of Isaiah, ' With joy you will draw water from the wells of salvation ' (Isaiah 12. 3). When he got back the Temple courts were packed with people. The High Priest then took the water and poured it out on the great altar. No doubt it was all a thanksgiving for water, which had been so scarce on the desert journeyings, and perhaps also it was a kind of acted prayer that the rain would not fail. But think of it. The crowds, the water poured out on the altar—and then, perhaps at that precise moment Jesus rises and cries, ' You are thanking God for the water from which, if you drink, you will thirst again. Come to me and I will give you the water which will quench for ever the thirst of your souls.' It was in the very situation that Jesus found his picture and his metaphor, and the thing becomes alive.

But on that same day there was another ceremony late in the evening. In the Temple courts there had been prepared great candelabra, and once again the courts were crowded with people. On that day alone it was forbidden that anyone in Jerusalem should light any light at evening until a given signal. The signal was the lighting of the great candelabra in the Temple. At the given time they were lit, and suddenly the dark, shadowed Temple courts blazed into light; and at that, light after light appeared all over the city, and all the darkness was lit up. And it was just at that moment that Jesus cried, ' I am the light of the world. These lights of yours will light the city streets; but I light the way of life and the way to eternal life.'

Once again Jesus took his picture from that which was

happening at that very moment—and how vivid and dramatic it must have been.

Let us take another example—this time one which will be well known to most of you. One of the most awe-inspiring sights in the Gospel stories is to see Jesus angry, and we see that on the occasion when Jesus drove the money-changers and the sellers of victims from the Temple courts (*Matthew 21. 12, 13; Marks 11. 15-17; Luke 19. 45, 46; John 2. 13-17*). What was it in that situation that roused the wrath of Jesus?

Every adult Jew had to pay the yearly Temple tax. It was half a shekel, that is, about two shillings. That sum does not seem much to an affluent society, but it has to be evaluated in the light of the fact that in Palestine at that time a working man's wages were eightpence a day, and therefore this tax was equal to three days' wages; clearly, quite a demand. This was generally paid in the week before Passover time. Just before that booths were set up, in all the towns and villages, and it could be paid there, but by far the largest amount of payments were made in the Temple court by pilgrims who had come to the Passover Festival. Now that Temple tax could only be paid either in half shekels of the treasury or in Galilaean half shekels. Ordinarily in Palestine all kinds of currency were valid—Greek, Roman, Egyptian, Tyrian, Phoenician, Syrian. But the reason for this special demand was that all other currencies had the head of a king or emperor stamped on them, and were therefore in the eyes of the Jews graven images.

So in the Temple courts there were the tables of the

money-changers who would provide the right kind of currency—a useful service one would think. But there was a catch in it. For every coin they changed these money-changers charged one *ma'ah* which was the equivalent of two pence; and, if the coin the pilgrim offered was of a high denomination, and if thus change was necessary the pilgrim had to pay another *ma'ah* to get his change. So the situation was that the unfortunate pilgrim was likely to have to pay an extra fourpence to have his coin changed and to get his change—and remember that was another half day's wages. It was a sheer ramp; it was a fleecing of the poor and humble pilgrims, and it brought into the Temple treasury many thousands of pounds extra each year.

But there were also the sellers of victims. Most visits to the Temple involved some kind of sacrifice; and the commonest sacrifice for the poor people consisted of pigeons and doves. All sacrifices had to be examined to see that they were without spot or blemish, and Temple inspectors were to make the examination. It was perfectly possible to buy your doves or pigeons outside the Temple, but, if you did, you could be quite certain that the inspector would find a blemish in it. He would then say, ' You would be better to buy from our Temple shops; the victims have all been examined there, and that will save you a lot of trouble.' Again it looked like a useful service, but outside the Temple a pair of pigeons would cost as little as ninepence, and inside the Temple at the official booths a pair of pigeons could, and often did, cost as much as fifteen shillings. Once again it was a flourishing ramp at the expense of the poor pilgrims. It brought into the Temple authorities as much as £70,000 a year. And these booths were called the Bazaars of Annas, because they were the personal business property of Annas the High Priest. That is why, as John tells the story, Jesus after his arrest was brought first to Annas (*John 18. 13*), so that Annas might have an opportunity to gloat over the downfall of this reckless young Galilaean who had tried to upset his vested interest.

When Jesus drove these money-changers and these sellers of victims out of the Temple courts, it was a blow for social justice. And there was something else. All this was going on in the Court of the Gentiles. There were three other courts in the Temple, the Court of the Women, the Court of the Israelites, and the Court of the Priests. But beyond that Court of the Gentiles the Gentiles could not go. In fact to go beyond it was for a Gentile a crime punishable by death. The one place in which the Gentile might pray and meditate and perchance find God had become a place where there was buying and selling and huckstering so that worship had become impossible. Jesus was angry with those who made it impossible for others to worship God.

Let us take one more example. In the Revelation the saying of the Risen Christ to the Church at Laodicea is (*Revelation 3. 15-18*), 'I know your works; you are neither hot nor cold. Would that you were cold or hot! So because you are lukewarm and neither cold nor hot, I will spew you out of my mouth. For you say, I am rich, I have prospered, and I need nothing; not knowing that

you are wretched, pitiable, poor, blind and naked. Therefore I counsel you to buy from me gold refined by fire,
that you may be rich, and white raiment to clothe you
and to keep the shame of your nakedness from being
seen, and salve to anoint your eyes that you may see.'
There is not a sentence in that letter which does not arise
directly from the situation in Laodicea.

Laodicea is neither hot nor cold, so that the very sight
of her makes a man want to be sick. Laodicea was a spa
with medicinal springs, and, however medically curative
these springs may be, they often have a smell and a taste
which are repulsive and disgusting. Laodicea well knew
about the waters which are neither hot nor cold and which
make a man want to be sick.

Laodicea claimed to be rich and prosperous and to
need nothing. Laodicea was one of the wealthiest cities
in the world. It was the banking centre of Asia Minor.
When Cicero was travelling in Asia Minor he cashed his
letters of credit there. But the point is this. Laodicea in
the latter part of the first century was devastated by a
terrible earthquake which left the city in ruins. The
Roman government offered help towards rebuilding, but
the city authorities said they did not need it and could do
their own rebuilding. Laodicea was actually the city which
said, 'I need no help. I can run life for myself.' But the
Risen Christ says to her, ' However rich you may be in
earthly wealth in the sight of God you are poverty-
stricken.'

The risen Christ counsels Laodicea to buy white raiment that the shame of her nakedness may be clothed.

In the pasture lands around Laodicea there grazed a kind of sheep with a glossy black fleece which was unique in the world. And therefore Laodicea was a centre of the clothing trade. There was, in fact, a short black jacket made of these famous fleeces which was called throughout the world a 'Laodicean.' So the risen Christ says to Laodicea, 'You may be famous all over the world for the clothes that you produce. But in the sight of God your soul is naked.'

The risen Christ advises Laodicea to buy salve to anoint her eyes that she might see. Laodicea was famous as the centre of eye treatment in the ancient world. There was produced there an eye salve which people came from all over the world to buy. But the Risen Christ says to her, 'You may think that you can cure the blindness of men's eyes, and maybe so you can as far as their physical sight is concerned, but you are spiritually completely blind, and only I can cure you.'

It is easy to see that the understanding of the letter depends entirely on the understanding of the historical background against which it is written. Certainly, if we are to communicate the true meaning of scripture, the historical approach is completely necessary.

iv. The fourth approach necessary to communicate the New Testament is the *psychological* approach. The psychological approach involves the investigation of, not only what people did, but why they did it. It has, of course, to be said that psychology is not an exact science in the sense that history and linguistics are; but, nonetheless, there can be illumination here.

67

Take, for instance, the question, Why did Judas betray Jesus? Why should anyone wish to betray the loveliest person who ever lived? When we probe into the motives of this, certain possibilities emerge.

(*a*) Iscariot could mean *ish kerioth*, man of Kerioth. If Judas was the man of Kerioth he was the only non-Galilaean in the Twelve, the only lowlander in a group of highlanders. It may be that from the first he was the odd man out and so became soured and embittered, until love turned to hate.

(*b*) It may be that Judas quite simply turned king's evidence, that he saw that the ship was sinking, that the end was inevitable, and that he sought to save his own skin, before the crash came.

(*c*) It may be that he could not stand the eyes of Jesus. It seems that quite early Jesus saw the degeneration of Judas. ' Did I not choose you, the twelve,' he said, ' and one of you is a devil?' (*John 6. 70*). The others did not see through Judas, or quite certainly he would not have been allowed to do what he did—they would have killed him first. But Jesus knew, and every time he looked at Jesus, Judas knew that Jesus knew. At the end he could stand it no longer, and betrayed him, to get rid of the man who could see into his soul.

(*d*) It may be that Judas betrayed Jesus for the sake of money. He was, as John tells the story (*John 12. 6*), the treasurer of the apostolic band, and he pilfered from the funds. It may be that it was simply avarice that made Judas betray Jesus. If he did, it was the most dreadful bargain in history, for he sold Jesus for thirty pieces of silver, precisely the ordinary price of a slave in the market-place.

(e) It may be that Judas betrayed Jesus because he was bitterly disappointed. The word Iscariot may well be a form of the Latin word *sicarius*, in Greek *sikarios*., both of which mean a dagger-bearer. These dagger-bearers were violent nationalists, pledged to war to the knife against the Romans, and prepared to carry on a career of murder and assassination to get their way. It may be that Judas saw Jesus with the power of his words as a great national leader who could at last blast the Romans and lead the Jews to power. And it may be that, when he saw Jesus refusing the way of political power and taking the way to the Cross, he was so bitterly disappointed that love turned to hate, and he betrayed the man who, as he saw it, had failed him and won him under false pretences and had let him down.

(f) But I think that there is another view of Judas, the view which de Quincey once put forward. I think that it is likely that Judas never meant Jesus to die. This view starts from the same point as the last view. Judas was the violent political nationalist. He saw Jesus as the political hope and saviour of the nation. But Jesus was taking no steps to be the leader Judas wanted him to be. And so Judas betrayed Jesus, not to have him killed, but to force his hand. He wanted to put Jesus into a position when he would be compelled to act, even if for no other reason, than to save his life. And Jesus did not act, and Judas saw that his whole plan had gone tragically and disastrously wrong.

69

F

What makes that so likely is the story itself. If Judas had simply wished to betray Jesus, he ought to have rejoiced in his capture. But what did Judas do? He went to the priests and flung their money back at them, and went out and committed suicide, for his plan had ended in tragedy.

The basic mistake of Judas was that he wanted Jesus to be, not what Jesus is, but what he wanted him to be.

It is clearly a fascinating study to try to see, not only what the people in the New Testament did, but also to see why they did it, and the more our knowledge of the background of the story, the better our chance to work this out.

v. Lastly, we must make the *devotional* approach to the New Testament. In the last analysis our only reason for studying the New Testament is that we may see Jesus more clearly, and love him more dearly, and follow him more nearly.

It is told that once at a dinner party after the guests had dined and wined, it was suggested that each should recite something. There was a famous actor there, and, when his turn came, he recited the 23rd Psalm with all the resources of oratory and elocution. He sat down to a storm of applause. The next to rise was an undistinguished little man. He, too, began to say the 23rd Psalm, and at first there was a murmur of surprise and a titter of amusement that he should seek to compete with the great actor. But before he had recited a verse there was complete stillness and silence, and when he sat down there was no applause, only the silence that is more eloquent than applause. And when the little man had ended, the great actor turned to him. ' Sir,' he said, ' I know the psalm, but you know the shepherd.'

Here is the reason for the study of the New Testament, not that we should know the history or the linguistics or anything else, but that we should know him of whom it tells; for we can never communicate Jesus Christ to others, until we know him ourselves.

CHAPTER 4

THE GOSPEL IN TRADITION

WE can never even begin to understand the Bible, unless we first realise that our attitude to it can only be expressed in a series of paradoxes, and that in each case to overstress one arm of the paradox can only end in a mistaken view. We may begin by looking at three of these paradoxes.

i. In one sense the Bible must be open to all, and in another sense it is dangerous that it should be so. Two famous statements were made by Tyndale and Erasmus. Tyndale said: ' If God spare my life, ere many years I will cause a boy that driveth the plough shall know more of Scripture than thou dost.' And he was speaking to ' a learned man.' Erasmus wrote in the preface to his Greek New Testament of 1516:

' I totally disagree with those who are unwilling that the Holy Scriptures translated into the common tongue should be read by the unlearned. Christ desires his mysteries to be published abroad as widely as possible. I could wish that even all women should read the Gospel and St. Paul's Epistles, and I would that they were translated into all the languages of all Christian people, that they might be read and known not merely by the Scots and the Irish but even by the Turks and the Saracens. I wish that the farm worker might sing them at the plough,

that the weaver might hum them at the shuttle, and
that the traveller might beguile the weariness of the
way by reciting them.'

Tyndale and Erasmus write of the dream of Scripture
being open and available to every man. On the other hand,
it is told that in the First World War the Quakers volun-
teered for services in connection with the wounded. The
Quakers, being pacifists, could not fight but this they
could do. The government knew the Quaker position, and
accepted their services on condition that they did not
preach. The Quakers agreed not to preach, but asked if
they might be allowed simply to read passages from the
Bible to wounded men. The answer was that they were
to be allowed to do this, but it had to be borne in mind
that in certain circumstances the Bible can be a highly
dangerous book.

Both attitudes are right. It is of the very essence of the
faith as the Protestant Church sees it that the Bible should
be an open book to all men, and yet it is of the very essence
of the Bible that it can be a very dangerous book. That is
one of the paradoxes of the Bible.

ii. There is a second paradox of the Bible. Protestantism
involves the acceptance of the principle that the Bible is
the 'supreme rule of faith and life.' The *First Helvetic
Confession* (1536) lays it down: 'Canonic Scripture, the
word of God, given by the Holy Spirit and set forth to the
world by the prophets and apostles, the most perfect and
ancient of all philosophies, alone contains perfectly all
piety and the whole rule of life.' Chillingworth said: ' The

Bible and the Bible alone is the religion of Protestants.'
There will be few who will deny that the Bible is the
supreme rule of faith and life.

And yet—and this is the other arm of the paradox—
it is the simple and inescapable fact that the faith is prior
to the Bible as a whole. It was not the New Testament
which begat the faith, but the faith which begat the New
Testament. The New Testament in its complete form does
not emerge until the Festal Letter of Athanasius in A.D.
346. Of course, the writing of it had been completed long
before that; but it is not until then that the contents of
the New Testament are listed as they are today. But,
apart from that, no part of the New Testament was written
at the earliest earlier than A.D.60, and its writing was not
completed until perhaps as late as A.D.120. It is the simple
historical fact that there was a Church long before there
was a New Testament, and in the end it was the Church
which defined that of which the New Testament should
consist, and even today there exist books which were on
the fringe of the New Testament, and even some which in
certain places were for a time accepted as Scripture. The
Muratorian Canon, for example, the first 'official' list of
New Testament books, dating back to about A.D.180,
includes the *Wisdom of Solomon*, and indicates that the
Apocalypse of Peter and the *Shepherd of Hermas* were accepted
by some. It is by decision of the Church that the books
called the apocryphal books are Scripture for the Roman
Catholic Church but not for the Protestant Church. When
Luther issued his New Testament, he listed at the end of
the contents in a kind of separate list five books—*Hebrews*,

2 *Peter*, *Jude*, *James* and the *Revelation*—which were not to him on a level with the other books.

Here then is the curious paradox. The Bible is the supreme rule of faith and life for the Church, yet the Church is historically prior to the New Testament. The New Testament is the judge of the Church, yet the Church was the judge of what the contents of the New Testament should be. There is very clearly a complicated relationship between Bible and Church.

iii. There is still a third paradox. The implication of the sayings of Tyndale and of Erasmus with which we began have clearly as their implication that the simplest person can read the Bible and profit from that reading. And so indeed it has been. In 1563 Foxe wrote of the situation when Wicliffe's translation first became available: '. . . Some gave five marks (about £40), some more, some less for a book: some gave a load of hay for a few chapters of St. James or of St. Paul in English . . . To see their travails, their earnest seekings, their burning zeal their readings, their watchings, their sweet assemblies . . . may make us now in these days of free profession to blush for shame.' Clearly, the Bible did speak to the ordinary man.

F. C. Grant (*How to Read the Bible*, p. 11) tells a story of that very great scholar Adolf Harnack. When Harnack was at the height of his fame as a theological teacher in Berlin, he heard of a rumour which said that he had said that ' no one in Berlin understands the Bible except the great Professor Harnack.' The next day he went into his lecture with an audience of five hundred students gathered to hear him. He referred to the rumour and then he said: 'Many a chambermaid in this vast city, reading her Bible at her bedside after a long day's work, understands the Bible far better than the great Professor Harnack.'

This in one sense is true. And yet it is also true that there have been more books written about the Bible than about any other book. That flood of books still continues to flow. Everywhere groups gather to study the Bible. In schools and colleges and seminaries and universities the greatest scholars bring the finest scholarly equipment to the study and the elucidation and the exposition of the Bible. Here is a book written in alien languages, moving in a civilisation thousands of years away from ours, using categories of thoughts which are strange and alien to us, and therefore a book which will only yield its true fulness to the most intense study.

The Bible is at one and the same time a book from which the simplest mind can draw help for time and for eternity, and the deepest study cannot exhaust.

iv. We may look at one further paradox of Scripture. The Christian will begin with the assumption and the conviction that Scripture is the inspired word of God. This is the word of God. The question then arises (A. Harnack, *Bible Reading in the Early Church* p.9), is Scripture translatable and interpretable at all? Is it possible to translate that which is the word of God at all? When it is altered in translation is it not altered as the word of God? Can you interpret the word of God at all? Does the word of God not say: ' Thus says the Lord,' and to add anything to it is then to add something to the word of God—which is impossible; or it is to explain the meaning of the word of God—which only God can do.

How can this problem be explained? From very early times the Church has translated the Scriptures; from very early times the Church has made it her business to expound and to interpret the Scriptures, and yet, since the Scriptures are the word of God, they might be thought to be both untranslatable and uninterpretable. The only solution must be that the Scriptures must and can be translated and interpreted by the work of the same Spirit who originally inspired and wrote them. And this is to say that such translation and interpretation must be done within the Church, for the Church is the dwelling place of the Holy Spirit. And so once again we have arrived at the indissoluble connection between the Scriptures and the Church. And it is precisely this connection with which we are concerned, when we speak about the Bible and Tradition.

We shall first of all look very briefly at the background of Scripture, particularly in New Testament times. Here we shall find two opposite backgrounds. In the Greek background the sacred Scriptures of the Greek Mystery Religions were secret. Their contents were revealed only to the initiate, and then only after long preparation. The whole apparatus of the Mystery Religions was in fact so secret that none of its devotees ever did reveal it, and the oath which the initiate took was so terrible that even Nero, who must have been the most conscienceless of men, came to Eleusis for initiation and then refused to be initiated because the oath terrified him (Suetonius, *Nero* 34. 4). So then in Greek religion the sacred books were also secret books.

In Jewish religion precisely the opposite was the case. The Jewish Scriptures were open to all, and the study of them was the business and the obligation of all. ' This book of the law shall not depart out of your mouth, but you shall meditate upon it day and night ' (*Joshua* 1. 8). In the dreadful days of Antiochus Epiphanes the persecutors went from house to house searching for copies of the Law, and killing those who possessed them (*I Maccabees* 1. 55 *ff*).

Such restrictions as Judaism had were simply instances of practical common sense. Gregory Nazianzen approved of the practice of the Jews in not allowing every man at every age to read the whole of Scripture. The young were to read only those parts of Scripture which were to be taken literally, and about the meaning of which there was no dispute; not until a man reached the age of twenty-five was he to be allowed to read the whole Old Testament (Gregory Nazianzen, *Oration*, 2. 48). Origen writes that Jewish teachers held that the *Song of Solomon* should not be put into the hands of any man until he had reached years of maturity (Origen, *Prologue to the Song of Songs*). But these are merely practical details. As a matter of principle the Jewish Scriptures were wide open to any Jew, and the Jews were not only allowed to read them; they were commanded to do so.

When we examine the use of the Bible in the early Church, we find that there are two parallel streams. In the one stream, the Bible is an open book to everyone, without let or hindrance. It is available to all; and it is read by all; and the only complaint is that it is not read widely enough. In the other stream, both the reading of the Bible and the interpretation of the Bible are subject to certain controls. And the control is the faith and the rule and the tradition of the Church. It is to be noted at the beginning that these two points of view are not mutually exclusive; they can frequently both be found in the writings of one person. We shall begin by citing the main evidence for each of them. That evidence is well set out in Harnack's *Bible Reading in the Early Church*.

First then, we look at the point of view from which the Bible is the open book, available to all without restriction or even control, the book which the member of the Church from childhood upwards is urged to read, the book which is readily available to the pagan as well as to the Christian.

In the New Testament itself such references as there are to the reading of Scripture are to its public reading. The instruction to Timothy is: ' Till I come, attend to the public reading of scripture, to preaching, to teaching ' (*I Timothy 4. 13*). The Revelation begins with the blessing: ' Blessed is he who reads aloud the words of this prophecy ' (*Revelation 1. 3*). But obviously at the stage when the New Testament was being written the New Testament was not there to be read, and we have to proceed to the fathers for our main material.

' You know the holy scriptures,' Clement of Rome writes, ' your knowledge is praiseworthy, and you have deep insight into the oracles of God ' (Clement of Rome, *I Corinthians 53*). Barnabas insists that all Christians must be instructed in Scriptures, and must search out what the Lord has to say to them (*Letter of Barnabas* 21. 6). Polycarp writes to the Church at Philippi: ' I trust that you are well trained in the holy Scriptures' (Polycarp, *Philippians* 12). The second Letter of Clement has it: ' I believe that you are well aware that the living Church is the body of Christ, and that the books (that is, the Old Testament) and the Apostles regard the Church not as a temporal and earthly phenomenon, but as one that has come from above' (*Second Clement* 14).

Increasingly it is insisted that the Bible must be studied at home. According to Origen, it should be read for at least one or two hours every day at home, and even that is little enough (*Homily 2 on Numbers*). Clement of Alexandria suggests that the best time for reading is when the family are gathered for the principal meal of the day (*Pædagogos* 3. 12. 87). Both Clement of Alexandria and Tertullian recommend that husband and wife should study the Scripture and read the Bible together, and one of Tertullian's objections to marriage with a pagan is that in such a marriage such Bible reading is not possible (Clement of Alexandria, *Pædagogus* 2. 10. 96; Tertullian, *Ad Uxorem* 2. 6). Jerome insists on the reading of a fixed portion each day (*Letters* 54. 11; 107, 9). Many of the fathers recommend reading the Bible after the main meal, that is, before going to rest for the night (Chrysostom, *Homily I on Lazarus*). Jerome writes with a curious metaphor: ' When you eat your meals, reflect that you must immediately afterwards pray and read. Have a fixed number of lines of holy scripture, and render it as your task to your Lord. On no account resign yourself to sleep until you have filled the basket of your breast with a woof of this weaving' (Jerome, *Letters 54. 11*). Caesarius suggested that, if busy people could find no other time, they should read the Bible during meals (*Sermon 141;* this sermon is included among Augustine's sermons). Chrysostom insists that the Bible is to a Christian what his tools are to the artisan, and that therefore the poorest must buy one, and, if that is absolutely impossible, he must make up for it by listening most carefully to the readings in Church (*Homily II on John*). Chrysostom was eager to establish the custom that the passages of Scripture read in Church should be read again at home, and it was his regular custom to announce the readings for the next Sunday so that the congregation might study them and think about them before they came to Church. Bible study ' with wife and children,' and bible study intimately connected with public worship were urged by Chrysostom (*Homily 5 on Matthew; Homily 3 on Lazarus*).

Both Chrysostom and Jerome strongly criticise and rebuke those who had in their homes the most elaborately printed and bound bibles, on purple parchment, in gold ink, with gem-encrusted bindings, bibles which were never opened, and which were kept for display purposes and not for use. The little Paula is to have manuscripts of the holy Scriptures, ' but let her think less of gilding and Babylonian parchment and arabesque patterns than of correctness and accuracy of punctuation ' (Jerome, *Letters 107. 12*). ' Parchments are dyed purple, gold is melted into lettering, manuscripts are decked with jewels, while

Christ lies at the door naked and dying' (Jerome, *Letters* 22. 32).

Everything was done to help Bible study. Wealthy men like Pamphilus paid to have Bibles copied and given to the poor (Jerome, *Against Rufinus* 1. 9). Bible Classes and communal readings were arranged by neighbours in each other's houses. ' A man,' says Chrysostom, ' ought to call his neighbours together and read the Bible with them ' (*Homily 6 on Genesis*). Churches had libraries in separate buildings where there were copies of the Bible that all could read (Paulinus of Nola, *Letters 32*).

In particular children were carefully instructed in the Bible. Origen's father made him read and learn a part of the Bible by heart each day, a task which for the boy was a delight (Eusebius, *The Ecclesiastical History* 6. 2. 6). *The Apostolic Constitutions* lays it down (4. 11): ' Teach your children thoroughly the word of the Lord . . . and place in their hands every book of holy Scripture.' Even if they do not understand it, the very sound of it, and even the very contact with it, will leave its mark for good. The little Paula is to be given a set of box wood letters with which to make words, and let the Biblical names, for instances, the names in the genealogies of Christ, be the words she forms (Jerome, *Letters* 107. 4). Even the scheme of Paula's Scripture reading is laid out. She is to begin with the Psalms, and then to go on to the Proverbs of Solomon. She must then read Ecclesiastes to learn to despise the world. After that she can read the Gospels, and then the Acts and the Epistles. Then the Old Testament from Genesis to Judges; then Kings and Chronicles, the prophets, Ezra and Esther, and only then at the very end the Song of Songs, for only then will she know that book for what it really is.

There is to be constant learning by heart. Eusebius tells of a blind Egyptian called John. ' He possessed whole books of the holy scriptures, not on tables of stone, as the Apostle says, nor on skins of beasts nor on paper, which moth and time can devour, but . . . in his heart, so that, as from a rich literary treasure, he could ever as he wished repeat passages from the Law and the Prophets, now from the historical books, now from the Gospels and the apostolic epistles' (Eusebius, *Concerning the Palestinian Martyrs 13*).

The place that the Bible had in the Christian life and community was well known to the heathen, and the Diocletian persecution was a persecution of the Bible (Augustine, *Against Crescens 3. 26*). It was the demand that Christians should hand over their copies of the Scriptures to be burned (Eusebius, *The Ecclesiastical History 8. 2*). Sometimes the Christians succeeded in hiding them. In the *Acts of Agape and Chionia* the women tell how they have not been able to read the Scriptures since they hid them. ' It was the sorest grief to us that we could no longer read the Scriptures day and night, as we were ever accustomed to do until last year, when we hid them.'

There is every evidence that the Scriptures were wide open to the Christians and in the hands of all.

It is equally significant that the Christian Scriptures were wide open to the outsider, and that the Christian writers and apologists often invite their opponents to read the Scriptures and sometimes can even assume that they have read them. In the New Testament itself we find the Ethiopian reading the Scriptures (*Acts* 8. 28). Aristides, the earliest of the apologists, invites his heathen readers, first, to read his own work, and, then, to take the Scriptures into their hands and read them for themselves (Aristides, *Apology 16*). Justin Martyr says of the Scriptures to the heathen: 'We not only read them without fear, but we also offer them to you for study' (Justin, *First Apology 44*). Athenagoras in his Apology assumes that the Emperor Hadrian had read the Scriptures of the Old Testament (Athenagoras, *Embassy 9*). Justin knows that the Trypho with whom he was arguing had read and knew the Christian books (Justin Martyr, *Dialogue with Trypho 10, 18*). As for Celsus whose attack on Christianity Origen met, he can say of the Christian Scriptures: 'I know all' (Origen, *Against Celsus 1. 12*).

It was in fact the availability of the Scriptures which was a frequent cause of conversion. Tertullian speaks of the books which the Christians make no attempt to hide, and 'which many a chance throws into the hands of outsiders' (Tertullian, *Apology 31*). There are at least five recorded cases in which it was an encounter with the Scriptures which was the means of conversion.

It was to the writings of the prophets that Justin Martyr attributed his conversion. Justin was a man who came to Christianity after a long voyage through all the philosophies, and to the end of the day he wore the philosopher's robe. After he had tried them all, he happened on the writings of the prophets; he had begun with the

Stoic who was unable to lead him any nearer God; he went on to the Peripatetic, a shrewd man, who entertained him for a few days and then asked him to settle his fee that their intercourse might not be unprofitable. He went on to the Pythagorean who told him that he must begin with a working knowledge of music, astronomy and geometry; he went on to the Platonist who promised him the vision of God; and at the end of this intellectual odyssey he was no farther on. And then he found the prophets: ' There existed,' he says, ' long before this time certain men more ancient than all those who are esteemed philosophers, both righteous and beloved by God, who spoke by the Divine Spirit, and foretold events which would take place, and which are now taking place. They are called prophets. They alone both saw and announced the truth to men, neither reverencing nor fearing any man, not influenced by a desire for glory, but speaking those things alone which they saw and which they heard, being filled with the Holy Spirit. Their writings are still extant, and he who has read them is very much helped in his knowledge of the beginning and the end of things, and of those matters which the philosopher ought to know ' (*Dialogue with Trypho* 6).

Tatian was another who went through the whole gamut of heathen philosophy. He writes: ' While I was giving my most earnest attention to the matter, I happened to meet with certain barbaric writings, too old to be compared with the opinions of the Greeks, and too divine to be compared with their errors; and I was led to put faith in these by the unpretending cast of their language, the inartificial character of the writers, the foreknowledge displayed of future events, the excellent quality of the precepts, and the declaration of the government of the universe as being centred in one Being. And, my soul being taught of God, I discerned that the former class of writing lead to condemnation, but that these put an end to the lavery that is in the world' (*Address to the Greeks* 29).

Theophilus of Antioch tells how he used to disbelieve the claims of the Christians. ' At the same time,' he said, ' I met with the sacred Scriptures of the holy prophets,' and he was convinced (Theophilus, *To Autolycus* 1. 14).

Athenagoras was one of the great scholars of antiquity and he became a Christian and wrote one of the greatest of the Apologies, *The Embassy for the Christians*. Philip of Side in his *Christian History* sketches the biography of Athenagoras:

' Athenagoras was the first director of the school at Alexandria; his *floruit* was about the time of Hadrian and Antoninus, to whom he dedicated his *Embassy* on behalf of the Christians. He was a man who professed Christianity while wearing the philosopher's gown and was a leading man in the Academic School. Before Celsus he planned to write against the Christians, but, reading the Holy Scripture to make his attack more telling, he was so won over by the Holy Spirit as to become like the great Paul a teacher and not a persecutor of the faith he was attacking.'

Victorinus tells how he came to the end of his searching: ' While my mind was dwelling on these things and on many like thoughts I chanced upon the books which according to the tradition of the Hebrew faith were written by Moses and the prophets and found in them words spoken by God the Creator testifying of himself: I am that I am, and again, He that is hath sent me unto you ' (*On the Trinity* 1. 5).

It is abundantly clear that the Scriptures were not only wide open to every member of the Christian Church, but that they were also readily available to any heathen, and that in fact many of the heathen had an intimate knowledge of them.

But we must now turn to the other stream. There is a line of thought in the early Church which, without ever abandoning the universal availability of the Scriptures, yet sees that there is need of some kind of control and of some kind of context in which the Scriptures are to be read and of some kind of authority. It is obvious that this stage had to be reached.

i. It was clear that young and immature entrants into the faith and the Church could not cope with the vastness and the depth of the bible and its documents. As Harnack puts it: ' In time it must, of course, have been more and more clearly seen that it was unwise to launch young and immature Christians rudderless upon the wide ocean of the Bible ' (A. Harnack, *Bible Reading in the Early Church*, p. 67). To meet this Cyprian constructed his famous *Testimonia*, which was what Harnack called ' a systematised collection of biblical quotations for the use of *tirones.*' This book would provide the young and the inexperienced Christian with the biblical evidence for the various articles of his belief. This was obviously a useful handbook, but it does not give any real control.

ii. The Bible is on any grounds a difficult book. Ambrose (*Concerning Paradise* 58) pictures the heathen coming to an Old Testament passage, like that which lays down the rule of an eye for an eye and a tooth for a tooth, or to a New Testament saying such as that which says that the offending right hand must be cut off and thrown away, and says that it is perfectly possible that, if such a man did not get right teaching and guidance, he was worse off after reading than if he had never read at all. Clearly, the reader of the Bible had need of instruction and explanation and guidance, or he would be left sometimes puzzled and bewildered and not infrequently seriously misled.

iii. But, above all, the rise of heresy made some kind of authority in the interpretation of the Bible a necessity. By the middle of the second century all kinds of heretics were offering their systems, and all of them were claiming that their systems were based on Scripture. They were making Scripture mean what they wished it to mean. They were reading their own beliefs into Scripture rather than listening to the word of God in Scripture. It became ever increasingly clear that some authority other than subjective individualism was necessary.

The process by which this authority of interpretation was worked out can be traced in four writers. In them we can trace the rise of that tradition in the light of which the Roman Catholic Church still says that Scripture must be interpreted.

The first is Irenaeus, whose main work was produced round about A.D. 180. He had to refute the Gnostic systems, with their elaborate stories of æons, and powers, and demons, and with their fantastic exegesis and interpretation of Scripture. They all claimed that they had the authority of Scripture; some of them claimed to have a special and unique revelation given to them alone. All of them talked of the special revelations of the Holy Spirit given to them. How were they to be met? How was the Church to decide which interpretations of Scripture were orthodox and which were heretical, which were of the essence of the faith and which destructive of the faith?

Irenaeus laid down the principle which is still the Roman Catholic principle of tradition. Jesus himself taught the true exegesis of Scripture. As Luke has it: 'Beginning with Moses and all the prophets, he interpreted to them in all the Scriptures the things concerning himself' (*Luke 24. 27*). Jesus taught the apostles the true interpretation and they passed it on, and therefore, 'the standard is the rule of faith as preserved in churches in the apostolic succession' (R. M. Grant, *A Short History of the Interpretation of the Bible, p. 54*). 'True knowledge is the teaching of the apostles, and the ancient order of the Church in all the world, and the form of the body of Christ according to the successions of the bishops, to whom they transmitted the Church that is in each place, which has come down even to us, guarded without the composition of writings by a very thorough treatment (the rule of faith), neither increased nor diminished. In it there is a reading without falsification, and a lawful and diligent exegesis of the Scriptures' (Irenaeus, *Against Heresies 4. 33. 8*). The deduction is obvious. If anyone wants to gain this true apostolic understanding ' he should read the Scriptures with the presbyters of the church' (Irenaeus, *Against Heresies 4. 32. 1*). There the apostolic doctrine is to be found.

The principle is simple and clear. The true tradition was given by Jesus to his apostles; through them it is given in the apostolic succession to the bishops; and therefore it is not possible to study and interpret Scripture correctly apart from that tradition and outside the Church.

The second figure in this process is Tertullian, whose work was done in North Africa about A.D.200. His most important book in this connection is *Concerning the Prescription of Heretics*. The word *Prescription* is being used by Tertullian in a technical Roman legal sense. It could happen that, when a case was to come up for trial, one of the parties might demand that a prior principle or question should be first settled. That prior question was the *prescription*. And it is, of course, obvious that it could happen that the settlement of a prescription left no case to answer. The prescription which Tertullian advances is perfectly straightforward—*the Scriptures are the exclusive property of the Church, and no one has any right to use them except the Church*. Tertullian has the same three fundamental principles as Irenaeus. First, Jesus came to reveal the truth. Second, he entrusted this truth to his apostles. Third, they transmitted it to the apostolic Churches. Therefore only the apostolic Churches possess the truth and the tradition (*The Prescription of Heretics 20, 21*).

So when the heretics use Scripture they are in fact trespassing on territory to which they have no right of access. So the Church will say to them: ' Who are you? When and whence did you come? As you are none of mine, what have you to do with that which is mine? By what right, Marcion, do you hew my wood? By whose permission, Valentinus, are you diverting the streams of my fountain? By what power, Apelles, are you removing my landmarks?' The bible is the property of the Church, properly bequeathed to it by the apostles. The Church has the title deeds; the Church is the true heir. The heretic is dispossessed and disinherited. The bible belongs to the Church (Tertullian, *The Prescription of Heretics* 37). The final authority is the Church and of the Church's tradition, received from the apostles, and transmitted through the apostolic succession. Tertullian was a lawyer by profession, and he settled the matter with a lawyer's clarity and lucidity.

The third figure is Augustine who wrote his *Concerning Christian Doctrine* in A.D.397. Augustine lays down two principles which decide what the correct interpretation is. The first is a magnificent principle, for ever valid:

' If it seems to anyone that he has understood the divine Scriptures or any part of them, in such a way that by that understanding he does not build up that double love of God and neighbour, he has not yet understood (*Concerning Christian Doctrine 1. 36. 40*).

The test of correct interpretation is that it issues in love of God and love of man. And there can be no finer rule than that. Augustine's second principle is in the main stream. If a man is troubled about the interpretation of Scripture, and if he has doubts, and if there appear to be alternatives facing him, then ' he must consult the rule of faith ' (Augustine, *Concerning Christian Doctrine* 3. 2). Once again the deciding factor is the tradition of the Church.

The fourth figure in this progression is the one in whom the whole progression reached its peak. His name is Vincent of Lerinum, and his work was called the *Commonitorium*, and was written in A.D.434. His principle is the principle which we have been following. He writes: ' The line of the interpretation of the prophets and apostles must be directed according to the norm of the ecclesiastical and Catholic sense ' (*Commonitorium* 2). He then asks the question: What is Catholic? and gives the famous answer: *Quod ubique, quod semper, quod ab omnibus*, that which has been believed *everywhere, always, and by everyone*. He quotes *I Timothy 6. 20:* ' O Timothy, guard the deposit, avoiding the profane novelties of words,' and then he goes on to say: ' If novelty is to be avoided, antiquity is to be held; if novelty is profane, antiquity is sacred.' On the face of it this would seem to mean that there can never be any development in truth. But Vincent explains that truth is like the human body, which develops and grows, but which remains the same. ' It is right for the original dogmas of the heavenly philosophy in the course of time to be cared for, shined, and polished; but it is wrong for them to be truncated, changed or mutilated ' (*Commonitorium 21, 23*). Scripture is to be interpreted ' accordi to the traditions of the universal Church and according to the rules of Catholic dogma.' And who was to decide what was the tradition of the Church? That tradition was to be found in the agreement of the fathers, in the decisions of the counsels, and above all its custodian was the Pope, the earthly head of the Church.

Here then is the final position—*Scripture is to be interpreted according to the tradition of the Church*. We may trace this in one last step. We may set it out as it appears in the article of the Council of Trent on *Scripture and Tradition*, which dates to 1546:

' The Holy, Ecumenical, and General Synod of Trent ... having this aim always before its eyes, that errors may be removed and the purity of the Gospel preserved in the Church, which was before promised through the prophets in the Holy Scriptures and which our Lord Jesus the Son of God first published by his own mouth and then commanded to be preached through his apostles to every creature as a source of all saving truth and discipline of conduct; and perceiving that *this truth and this discipline are contained in written books and unwritten traditions*, which were received by the apostles from the lips of Christ himself, or, by the same apostles, at the dictation of the Holy Spirit, and were handed on and have come down to us; following the example of the orthodox fathers, this Synod receives and venerates with equal pious affection and reverence all the books both of the Old and the New Testaments, since one God is the author of both, *together with the said traditions*, as well as those pertaining to faith as those pertaining to morals, as having been given either from the lips of Christ or by the dictation of the Holy Spirit and preserved by unbroken succession in the Catholic Church . . .'

Here in this statement the Bible and the tradition are put on a level, and it is not altogether unfair to say that it puts the Church above the Bible, for in the last analysis it is by the traditions of the Church that the Bible is to be interpreted.

We must now try to assess the position that tradition ought to have in the interpretation of Scripture.

i. The New Testament itself is the first to declare that the interpretation of Scripture cannot be based solely on the judgment of the individual person. ' First of all,' writes the author of Second Peter, ' you must understand this, that no prophecy of Scripture is a matter of one's own interpretation ' (2 *Peter* 1. 20). The judgment of the individual is not the final authority in any interpretation.

ii. Entirely to dispense with all that tradition has to offer would be the action of a folly and of an arrogance, hard to understand, and still harder to justify. No interpreter can reasonably disregard the accumulated scholarship and wisdom of the Church. No man in any sphere of scholarship begins from nothing; he humbly and gratefully enters into other men's labours; and the man who seeks to interpret Scripture should be grateful to God that he too can do this.

It is mainly in this sense that Irenaeus thought of the tradition of the Church, as Harnack sees it. What

Irenaeus was thinking about was 'the great deposit of correct interpretation which is given to, and is the secure possession of, him alone who is in communion with the presbyters, the leaders of the Catholic and Apostolic Church' (A. Harnack, *Bible Reading in the Early Church*, p. 54).

There is either an almost incredible arrogance or an almost unbelievable naïveté in the person who feels no need of any help in the interpretation of Scripture. F. C. Grant tells how on occasion a lecturer dealt with the difficulties and the problems and the methods and the techniques of Bible study. ' When he had finished, a bright, attractive young woman got up and said: " You don't need some one to tell you how to read the Bible. Open it anywhere, read three verses, make your mind a blank, and the Holy Spirit will do the rest!" ' (F. C. Grant, *How to Read the Bible*, p. 14). However pious that may sound, it is obvious how much it deprives itself of, and it completely fails to realise that the help and the strength and the guidance of the Holy Spirit are in the devoted labours of the scholars in the fields of linguistics and archaeology and history and many another subject. In the work of the scholar the Holy Spirit is always operative, and not to use such work is to deny oneself the help of the Spirit. Augustine in the preface to his work *Concerning Christian Doctrine* stresses the fellowship of learning. ' If men learn nothing by human means, love, which binds men together in the bond of unity, would have no opportunity to draw souls together in mutual converse and to blend them with one another.'

Jerome is stern in his condemnation of those who are consumed with the desire to teach before they have learned. ' The old saying is found true of them, although they have not the wit to speak, they cannot remain silent. They teach to others the Scriptures they do not understand themselves; and if they are fortunate enough to convince them, they take upon themselves airs as men of learning. In fact they set up as instructors of the ignorant before they have gone to school themselves' (Jerome, *Letters* 130. 17). He writes to Paulinus:

' The art of interpreting the Scriptures is the only one of which all men everywhere claim to be masters. To quote Horace again,

"Taught or untaught we all write poetry."

The chatty old woman, the doting old man, the wordy sophist, one and all take in hand the Scriptures rend them in pieces and teach them before they have learned them . . . They do not deign to notice what Prophets and Apostles have intended, but they adapt conflicting passages to suit their own meaning. as if it were a grand way of teaching—and not rather the faultiest of all—to misrepresent a writer's views and to force the Scriptures reluctantly to do their will . . . It is idle to try to teach what you do not know, and—if I may speak with some warmth—it is worse still to be ignorant of your ignorance (Jerome, *Letters* 53. 7).'

Completely to neglect tradition, or even to despise tradition would be the act of a man who had neither wisdom nor humility.

iii. In the last analysis it is necessary to have some touchstone of belief. There is a real sense in which a church is an exclusive institution. A man has to give allegiance to certain beliefs before he can become a member of it. Any society makes certain demands upon its members, and so must the church.

This means that there cannot be in the church a complete individualism in the interpretation of Scripture. In the convent at Erfurt one of Luther's teachers was John Nathin, and he was a teacher on whom Luther always looked back with gratitude. Nathin actively discouraged the independent study of Scripture. ' Brother Martin,' he said, ' let the Bible alone; read the old teachers; they give you the whole marrow of the Bible; reading the Bible simply breeds unrest.' And in the end he commanded Luther on his canonical obedience to refrain from bible study (T. M. Lindsay, *History of the Reformation* 1. *199, 200*).

Nathin's solution is not the solution, but it is true that men can emerge from the study of Scripture with the most diverse interpretations of the same passages. There comes somewhere a limit to independence, and a time when the Church has to say that something is totally at variance with the whole body of the faith.

iv. Nathin's advice to Luther brings us to the danger of tradition. The danger of tradition is that it may become, and at times did become, a substitute for the Bible. There have been times when the Church set tradition far above the Bible, and when it did in fact discourage, if it did not forbid, Bible study. The Roman Catholic Church would no longer hold anything like this, but in the bull *Unigenitus* in 1713 the following propositions were expressly condemned:

> ' It is useful and necessary at all times, in all places, and for every kind of person to study and to know the spirit, the piety and the mysteries of sacred scripture.
>
> The reading of sacred scripture is for everyone.
>
> The obscurity of the sacred word of God is not an excuse for the laity to excuse themselves from the reading of it.
>
> The Lord's Day ought to be sanctified by Christians by the reading of piety and above all of the sacred scriptures.
>
> To take the New Testament from the hands of Christians is to close for them the mouth of Christ.
>
> To forbid the reading of sacred scripture to Christians, especially of the Gospel, is to forbid the use of the light to the sons of the light, and to cause them to suffer a kind of excommunication.'

Let us repeat, these propositions were *condemned*.

It was in the same spirit that the Church for so long looked with grave suspicion on the translation of the Scriptures into the vernacular languages. The Convocation of Oxford, under Archbishop Arundel in 1408, laid it down:

> ' It is a dangerous thing as witnesses blessed St. Jerome to translate the text of holy scripture out of one tongue into another; for in translation the same sense is not always easily kept . . . We therefore decree and ordain that no man hereafter by his own

authority translate any text of the Scripture into English or any other tongue by way of a book pamphlet or treatise; and that no man read any such book, pamphlet or treatise now lately composed in the time of John Wycliffe, or since, or hereafter to be set forth in part or in whole, publicly or privately, upon pain of greater excommunication, until the said translation be approved by the ordinary of the place, or if the case so require by the council provincial. He that shall do contrary to this shall likewise be punished as a favourer of heresy and error.'

And it is a matter of history that Tyndale could find no place in all England to translate the Scriptures, that his bibles were burned as ' the devil's merchandise,' and that he too died at the stake.

There has been, I think, a misjudging of the Church here. Such enactments were not in the interests of keeping a priestly dictatorship; they came rather from the terror that heresy might arise if Scripture got freely into the hands of those unequipped to use it. That this fear too was wrong may well be argued, but such a fear is a very different thing from the desire to impose or to continue a priestly domination.

When tradition closed the Bible and forbade translation then it is hard to see how it can have been anything other than misused.

Harnack (*Bible Reading in the Early Church, pp. 3, 4*) has summarised the difference between the Protestant and the Roman Catholic Church as he saw it in his day:

' According to the Protestant view, the Bible is a free gift to the community and to the individual without restriction or reserve; while according to the Catholic view the Bible is in the possession of the organised Church, which is bound to administer her property, as also the means of grace, for the good of the individual, according to her own judgment, and in the spirit of strict yet loving parental care. According to the Protestant point of view the Holy Scriptures, and these only, are the ultimate source and norm of all Christian knowledge; while according to the Catholic view, tradition, together with the living word of the infallible Church, stands side by side with the Bible, as equal, indeed, in many aspects, as superior, to it in authority.'

The difference can be exaggerated, for the Protestant Church too has standards of orthodoxy which in the end she will apply to those who interpret the Bible, as indeed any Church must have.

There is such a thing as the tradition of the Church. Any man who neglects such tradition is both foolish and arrogant. But as the Protestant sees it, that tradition is always secondary to the Bible, and can never be used to introduce into the Christian faith that for which Scripture provides no evidence itself. For the Protestant tradition is rather the priceless accumulation of experience rather than the touchstone or the source of truth.

It will be well to try to set down what the Roman Catholic Church means by tradition—at least in so far as a Protestant understands it. In his article on Tradition in the *Encyclopaedia of Religion and Ethics* N. P. Williams rightly lays it down that tradition involves two things—*a deposit and depositories to whom the deposit is entrusted*.

So then it is held that Jesus, partly during his life-time on earth, and partly during the forty days between the Resurrection and the Ascension (*Acts 1. 2*) gave to his people a deposit and revelation of truth, in which all the great doctrines of the Church and all the sacraments are at least in germ contained. He further taught them how to interpret that which in existing Scripture they had received (*Luke 24. 44, 45*). Part of the revelation, and a supremely essential part, is that they were to be the new Israel, the *ecclesia*, the Church, founded on Peter (*Matthew 16. 18*). He himself is always present with them and always will be (*Matthew 28. 20*), and he has promised the Holy Spirit to lead them into all truth (*John 16. 13*).

The presence of Christ and the Spirit of Christ give the Church the necessary infallibility to maintain and to develop the tradition. In the second century two things emerged in the Church—the canon of Scripture and the earliest and simplest creeds. They too are protectors of the tradition.

The tradition as we have already said requires not only a deposit but also depositories. The apostles were the first depositaries; they are succeeded by the bishops; and the decisions of the bishops in general council continue the tradition. It was necessary and indeed it was inevitable that the idea of the depository should acquire a focus; and the Vatican Council of 1870 declared that the Pope was endowed with the same infallibility as the Church, when he was exercising his office as the supreme pastor and teacher of Christians. The position is summed up in the saying of Pius ix: 'I am tradition.'

When the Reformation came, the Protestant Church reacted mainly, not against the idea of a deposit. That it accepted. It reacted against the depositories; and there was in fact within the Church a corruption at that time which made such a reaction entirely understandable. In place of the depositories the Protestant Church set 'the Bible and the Bible alone'.

But this very action confronted the Protestant Church with two problems which it has never wholly solved. First, if the Bible and the Bible alone is the depository of revelation, and the supreme rule, who made it so? Who gave it this authority? Who put it in this place? The difficulty of the Protestant Church is that the Church is prior to the New Testament, and in fact defined the New New Testament. The position becomes acute when we remember that the Roman Catholic Church accepts the Apocrypha as Scripture and the Protestant Church does not, and the main scriptural warrant, for instance, for prayers for the dead is founded on the Apocrypha (2 *Maccabees* 12. 43-45).

The second difficulty is the extreme divisiveness of Protestantism. If the Bible is erected as the only authority, then each finds in it what he wishes. It did not take the Protestant Church long to discover this, and it had in the end virtually to make itself the judge of that with which a man emerged from the study of Scripture. So the Wurtemberg Confession lays it down: 'We believe and confess that . . . this Church has the right of judgment concerning all doctrines.' The Thirty-nine Articles of the Anglican Church holds both positions at the one time. They lay it down that Holy Scripture contains all things necessary to salvation, that the creeds are to be believed and accepted because they can be proved by warrants from Scripture, that General Councils may and have erred, and that their decisions are only valid when confirmed by scripture. But then it goes on to say that ' the Church . . . hath authority in controversies of the faith,' and is ' a witness and a keeper of Holy Writ.' And the Anglican theologian, Thorndike, writing in the 1840's, can say: ' That the indispensable mark of the true Church is the preaching of that word and that ministering of the sacraments which the tradition of the whole Church confineth the sense of the Scriptures to intend.' This is simply to say that in the end the tradition of the Church has to be called in.

Where then would the Protestant and the Roman Catholic Church differ regarding tradition?

i. The Protestant Church would in the end say that the tradition is not an independent thing, but is contained in Scripture. As N. P. Williams puts it in the article already referred to, the Protestant Church would hold that the function of the apostles as the guardians of the truth was purely temporary and ended at their death, that this function was not transmitted to any other body of men, but that these same apostles, before they died, were divinely inspired to write the New Testament, and that in it the tradition is contained.

It is in this way that the Protestant Church would take the word *tradition*, when it occurs in the New Testament with reference to the Christian faith. Paul writes to the Thessalonians: ' So, then, brethren, stand fast and hold to the *traditions* which you were taught by us, either by word of mouth or by letter' (2 *Thessalonians* 2. 15). They are to separate themselves from anyone not living ' in accord with the *tradition* that you received from us' (2 *Thessalonians* 3. 6). It is the command to Timothy: ' Guard the *deposit* that has been entrusted to you' (1 *Timothy* 6. 20). The Greek word for to pass on an oral tradition is *paradidonai*, and for to receive such a tradition *paralambanein*. These are distinctively the words of oral tradition, and these are the words which Paul uses in connection with the narrative of the Last Supper (*I Corinthians* 11. 23), and of the evidence for the Resurrection (*I Corinthians* 15. 1), two supremely important passages.

In all these passages the Protestant would say that the reference is to a time before the Gospels were written down, and when in fact the Christian tradition was nothing else but oral, and that it was precisely this very tradition which was written down in the New Testament itself. The Protestant would then hold that the Bible is the tradition.

ii. The Protestant Church would then go on to hold that the tradition can therefore never supersede the Bible. The tradition has gone wrong when it either disallows the reading of the Bible or forbids the translation of the Bible. The Bible stands above the tradition, if the tradition be taken to mean anything other than the Bible.

iii. The Protestant view would hold that the tradition cannot add anything to that which is already in Scripture, and that no doctrine of the Church can be a true doctrine which is not directly founded on Scripture. The Protestant Church would, for instance, say that the dogma of the Bodily Assumption of the Virgin Mary cannot be a true doctrine, because there is no evidence for it in Scripture.

iv. It has nonetheless to be admitted that there is still a place for tradition in Protestant thought. To take a simple example, in *John 1. 1*, we read in the Greek *theos en ho logos*. From the point of view of pure language that could be translated: ' The Word was a god,' but if anyone chose to translate it that way, the argument would be that the whole body of Christian tradition and the whole weight of the New Testament way of thought is utterly against it. The deciding factor is in fact the whole body of truth which the Church accepts.

The modern view of Scripture has made this general appeal to tradition even more necessary. We no longer regard the Bible as an arsenal of proof texts, nor could we support this or that doctrine or view by citing this or that text. We would know only too well that equal and opposite texts can readily be quoted. We would try to take the whole view of Scripture to each question and each problem, and therefore we do admit that there is a general tradition of Christian truth of which the Church is at one and the same time the servant and the guardian. The main difference in the two views is not that the one view denies tradition and the other accepts it. No sane and reverent person can ever think of studying Scripture, as it were, outside the Church. The difference is rather that the Roman Catholic view sets Scripture and tradition side by side, and for the Protestant Church tradition is in effect the sum total of Scripture, as the Church guided by the Holy Spirit understands it.